Refiguring Democracy

Spain has become a remarkable democratic laboratory in which millions of citizens are experimenting with new forms of political expression. This book examines the dynamics of this political laboratory, showing that the upheavals it is experiencing are likely in the near future to affect democracies elsewhere in the world. Examining the new means of participation that were established in fields in which digital communication tools enabled the launch of novel dynamics of political action, the reader will gain access to a comprehensive analysis of the reshaping and mutation process that has affected such fields as activism, political parties and political participation.

Using a case study of Spain between 2011 and 2015, the book focuses on the changes that have taken place in politics and communication in Spain, paying particular attention to the 15M movement and its disruptive, innovative strength in all matters related to politics and communication. The chapters cover political repertoires and the hybridisation of horizontal and vertical political logics; the appearance of new political parties; the establishment of monitoring mechanisms as an essential means of political expression and participation; and the subversion of rationality across media as a product of the communication strategies implemented by online political activism.

Showing that Spain is not just at the forefront of democratic innovation, but that it is a political laboratory in which trials are taking place that tell us much about the future of democracy everywhere, this book will be of great use to scholars of political theory, democracy and philosophy.

Ramón A. Feenstra is a lecturer in the Department of Philosophy and Sociology at the Universitat Jaume I de Castellón, Spain.

Simon Tormey is a professor at the School of Social and Political Sciences at the University of Sydney, Australia.

Andreu Casero-Ripollés is head of the Department of Communication Sciences and associate professor at the Universitat Jaume I de Castellón, Spain.

John Keane is Professor of Politics at the University of Sydney and at the Wissenschaftszentrum Berlin, Germany.

Routledge Studies in Anti-Politics and Democratic Crisis

Series Editors: Jack Corbett, University of Southampton and Matt Wood, University of Sheffield

This book series aims to provide a forum for the discussion of topics and themes related to anti-politics, depoliticisation, and political crisis. We supposedly live in an anti-political age in which popular disaffection threatens to undermine the very foundations of democratic rule. From the rise of radical right wing populism through to public cynicism towards politicians, institutions and processes of government are being buffeted by unprecedented change that have in turn raised questions about the viability of seemingly foundational practices. The series is intentionally pluralistic in its geographic, methodological and disciplinary scope and seeks works that push forward debate and challenge taken-for-granted orthodoxies.

For a full list of available titles please visit www.routledge.com/Routledge-Studies-in-Anti-Politics-and-Democratic-Crisis/book-series/RSAPDC.

Refiguring Democracy
The Spanish Political Laboratory
Ramón A. Feenstra, Simon Tormey, Andreu Casero-Ripollés and John Keane

Refiguring Democracy
The Spanish Political Laboratory

**Ramón A. Feenstra, Simon Tormey,
Andreu Casero-Ripollés and
John Keane**

Routledge
Taylor & Francis Group

LONDON AND NEW YORK

First published 2017 by Routledge

2 Park Square, Milton Park, Abingdon, Oxon, OX14 4RN

605 Third Avenue, New York, NY 10017

Routledge is an imprint of the Taylor & Francis Group, an informa business

First issued in paperback 2021

British Library Cataloguing in Publication Data
A catalogue record for this book is available from the British Library

Library of Congress Cataloging in Publication Data
A catalog record for this book has been requested

ISBN: 978-1-138-06368-6 (hbk)
ISBN: 978-1-03-217913-1 (pbk)
DOI: 10.4324/9781315160733

Typeset in Times New Roman
by Taylor & Francis Books

Contents

List of tables

Foreword

On the 15th May 2011, the whole of Spain was convulsed by one of the most spectacular popular uprisings in its history and in the history of the modern democratic world. Eight million Spanish citizens took part in the occupation of public squares and buildings in at least 60 towns and cities across the country. The movement of the *'indignados'* (or 'pissed off') was born. At the time, and still until today, Spanish citizens have had plenty to be disgruntled about: economic recession, high unemployment, endemic corruption, cronyism, wasteful and reckless 'megaprojects', mounting central and local government debt, and much else besides. With both major political parties complicit in these dynamics, the occupation by citizens of public spaces was seen by them as a necessary antidote to the 'business as usual' mantra offered by the cartel parties and mainstream media. 15M, as this uprising came to be called, revealed the power of the powerless: It demonstrated the capacity of multimedia savvy citizens to set in motion the search for a new democratic politics that aimed to overcome the decadence and disintegration of a dysfunctional political order.

This book sets out to map and analyse the extraordinary political experimentation that has been going on in Spain since 2011, and to ask whether the local democratic innovations are of global importance – for instance, by revealing the inherent limits of parliamentary representation and the birth of a new type of post-electoral politics. The book first appeared in Spanish as *La reconfiguración de la democracia. El laboratorio político español* (Feenstra, Tormey, Casero-Ripollés & Keane 2016). This slightly revised translation is a contribution to the Routledge Studies in Anti-Politics and Democratic Crisis series, which aims to provide a forum for unorthodox scholarship on how democracies caught up in deepening crises can best renew their spirit and substance. We wish to express our thanks to the series editors, Jack Corbett and Matt Wood, as well as the senior editorial assistant, Lydia de Cruz, for their encouragement and support. We warmly acknowledge the excellent work of our translator from the Spanish, Mary Savage; Trish Treagus, who so professionally edited and polished the English-language manuscript; and Lindy Baker, *genial coordinadora* of the Sydney Democracy Network (SDN) at the University of Sydney. We are grateful as well for the support and friendship of Professor Domingo García Marzá at the Universitat Jaume I de Castellón.

Our research and writing have been generously supported by grants from the Spanish Ministry of Economy and Competitiveness (FI2013–47136-C2–2-P and CSO201452283-C2–1-P); the Universitat Jaume I de Castellón (P1.1B2013–24); the BBVA Foundation Grants for Researchers, Innovators and Cultural Creators (2014); the School of Social and Political Science (SSPS) and the Sydney Democracy Network (SDN) at the University of Sydney. We owe special thanks to those citizens, civic networks and organisations that are the focus of our book, and who generously granted us interviews: *Plataforma Afectados por la Hipoteca* (PAH), *iai@flautas*, DRY, 15MpaRato and Attac; the members of a number of new political parties, including *Podemos, Partido X*, CUP, *Barcelona en Común, Castellón en Moviment, Valencia en Común, Escaños en Blanco* and *Partido Pirata*; and many scores of independent-minded citizens who spoke to us at length about their active involvement in efforts to renew public life under challenging economic and political conditions.

Ramón A. Feenstra
Simon Tormey
Andreu Casero-Ripollés
John Keane
Castellón and Sydney, December 2016

Introduction

For the past few years, the Spanish political scene has been going through complex and fiercely high-spirited times. Since 2009, data disclosed by the Centre of Social Research (CIS) have shown politicians and representation structures falling into disrepute. Politicians and political parties have been between the third- and fourth-highest causes of concern amongst citizens, with corruption in second place, since July 2013. The above data show a great deal of citizen disaffection, defined by a sense of cynicism and lack of trust towards the political representation process, as well as widespread disengagement from its core institutions (Alonso 2014). At the same time, new methods of political expression and participation have surfaced in the context of citizen disaffection with politics: camping events, demonstrations, civil gatherings to block evictions, novel monitory mechanisms, new political parties, independent media, proliferation of civil bodies for the defence of public services and popular legislative initiatives, among many others. Despite the growing disengagement and distance between the representative and represented groups, politics in Spanish social circles is livelier than ever. Such a context has enabled the establishment of an unprecedented democratic laboratory in the fields of experimentation and innovation in politics, making it an exceptional case study.

In political science, the term *participation* is generally – often exclusively – associated with representation structures (Verba & Nie 1972). The Spanish scene, however, is proof that experimentation has become the norm, not the exception, in all matters related to the means and methods of participation carried out by members of civil society. Currently, numerous examples show that participation is not limited to choosing those who join the government through elections or influencing their decisions. Participation goes beyond turning out to vote, joining a party or contacting one's political representatives; it is now expressed in numerous innovative ways – conventional or otherwise – in both the spheres of representative structures and of civil society (Baiocchi & Ganuza 2016; García Marzá 1998, 2008, 2013).

Our current situation seems to have witnessed the establishment of two key trends. On the one hand, there is a growing disaffection with some established the representation structures caused by a generalised disapproval of their methods, although the value of their existence is never denied. On the other hand, there is a growing demand for civil participation through new political forms among some citizen strata. The renowned claim *'no nos representan'* ('they do not represent us'), together with a demand for *democracia real* (real democracy), bring together two ideas: the disaffection with the existing situation and the vindication of the re-invention of some political forms that renovates and reshapes representative and participative mechanisms.

The current democratic scene is thus characterised by a growing tension, marked by the separation between the (de facto) key pillars of the representation process and our (normative) idea of an enriched and more dynamic democracy. In other words, there is a crisis of representation on one side and a craving for more citizen participation on the other.

Moreover, there is an important novelty: the consolidation of a broad range of new tools and means of communication. The appearance of a new communicative environment is causing essential changes in numerous fields, especially those related to politics and political communication, the dynamics and structures of which have been altered. New information banks and means of information spreading are flourishing; the private is rendered public; muckraking becomes normal; and public spheres, some of them in cross-border settings, become regular features of political life (Keane 2013). The proliferation of internet-based social media has enabled citizens to make use of technological tools with which they not only consume but also create content. Such an innovation has empowered the public, who are finding new autonomous spaces on the internet (Castells 2009; Jenkins 2006). The new 2.0 landscape, regardless of any potential issues therein (Chester 2007; Sunstein 2007; Hindman 2009), translates into an abundance of information over scarcity, the broadcast of news on a many-to-many basis over the classic one-to-many style, transparency over opacity, clarity over exclusivity and interactivity over passivity (McNair 2006). These changes are contributing to the design of new means of collective action, wherein connectivity plays a key role because of the internet (Bennett & Segerberg 2012). The internet is thus becoming a catalyst for political activism (Lomicky & Hogg 2010). Social media not only improves, potentially, the organisation, coordination, aggregation, orchestration, mobilisation and globalisation of citizen action and protest but also creates new methods of political action.

The new methods of action, in turn, renew and transform the political participation of civil society, which finds fresh alternatives, perspectives, tactics and repertoires surfacing around the notion of protest (Van Laer & Van Aelst 2010). In that sense, the Spanish context is a field of continued political experimentation, where the 15M movement triggered political innovation. From occupying public areas in 2011 to creating new political parties in 2013 and 2014, to bringing a series of civil initiatives and mechanisms to light, the participation in and use of new communication strategies, born in peripheral political contexts, has proved to be primarily active, open and ready for innovation. This movement, influenced by previous mobilisations (e.g. Iceland's pots and pans revolution and the Arab uprisings), encouraged protests by the *indignados* (the outraged) in numerous contexts (e.g. Occupy and Yo Soy 132). However, what is particularly notable about 15M is its ability to maintain a high level of commitment and participation on behalf of specific social strata over time. Political experimentation has become the main focus of the political lab.

The aim of this book is to examine and reflect on the new means of participation that were established in fields in which new digital communication tools enabled the launch of novel dynamics of political action. Throughout this book, the reader will gain access to a comprehensive analysis of the reshaping and mutation process that has affected fields such as activism, political parties and political participation. More specifically, the following topics will be examined: 1) political repertoires and the hybridisation of horizontal and vertical political logics; 2) the appearance of new political parties; 3) the establishment of monitoring mechanisms as an essential means of political expression and participation; and, lastly, 4) the subversion of rationality across media as a product of the communication strategies implemented by online political activism. Due to the relevance of these topics, we will dedicate a separate chapter to each. Thus, we hope to offer an overall view of the way democracy is being reshaped in the Spanish lab through the impact of social media, on one hand, and social and political changes, on the other.

This research was conducted through a case study of the Spanish setting between 2011 and 2015. The study is based on a combination of sources, such as in-depth interviews with activists, content analysis of journalist materials, websites, Facebook pages and Twitter updates. Additionally, extensive qualitative analysis was carried out over a considerably large number of national and international research projects, focusing on the changes that took place in politics and communication in Spain and paying particular attention to the 15M movement and its disruptive, innovative strength in all matters related to politics and communication. Different groups were interviewed from 2013 until 2015 in Barcelona, Madrid, Valencia and Castellón. The process involved heterogeneous groups of people who had taken part in any of the numerous 15M-based initiatives, the establishment of new political parties, or political activism in general. A total of 87 people were interviewed over 53 hours. The interviews were either one-to-one, in small groups, or were held in larger workshops to enable the free exchange of points of view. The reasons this book draws from theoretical studies, as well as case studies and interviews, are twofold. On one hand, the aim is to introduce and delve deeper into the key debates in the fields of democratic theory and political communication. Such an interdisciplinary approach is, in turn, due to the plural investigative trajectory of the four authors of this book as well as their conviction that an approach such as theirs can give a broader focus to a complex topic, such as the one dealt with here. On the other hand, the intention is to verify the theoretical and qualitative research carried out against the opinions of those who are playing major roles in the transformations taking place in the fields of activism and digital politics. The results presented in this book come from a very close collaboration between the University of Sydney, especially with the Sydney Democracy Network (SDN) and the School of Social and Political Sciences, and the Universitat Jaume I de Castellón, especially its Department of Philosophy and Sociology.

Throughout the following pages, we will enter the Spanish political lab to see how the outlines of democracy are changing – a task that stretches beyond the local context, as it could be announcing changes that could affect other democracies worldwide in the future. If we are right and Spain is at the avant-garde of political experimentation and innovation, this book could be instrumental in showing where and how democracy is currently evolving.

1 The transformation of political logics: beyond the 'horizontal' and the 'vertical'?

For scholars who are interested in different ways of 'doing politics', or the logics of participation, Spain post-15M offers an intriguing context ripe for analysis. During this period, the gap between the political class and the public has grown considerably, a distance that affects citizens' views of the political system and its cornerstones: political parties, parliament and elections. This distancing also affects civil society's expectations about the possibilities of transforming politics and improving democracy. Since 15 May 2011, there has been a constant stream of new initiatives, at first mainly in the form of street protests and mobilisations, but later reflected in the political institutionalisation of numerous platforms and new political formations. Demonstrations, occupations in public squares, actions to stop evictions, self-management initiatives, bank boycotts, popular legislation initiatives, protests outside politicians' homes (*escraches*) and the creation of new political parties are just some of the forms of political expression that have defined Spain's rich and complex political-activist ecosystem since 2011.

The complexity of these new political forms has been striking, as is the fact that Spain found itself on the front line of the dynamics of global capitalism. Spain's economic crisis coincided with a political crisis. The hallmarks of the Spanish economic crisis bore the imprint of the US and the UK cases, but they had local qualities (Pianta 2013). Spain, too, gorged itself on a diet of expanding credit during the 1980s and 1990s. Much of the credit assumed the form of housing loans and megaproject speculation, especially in the coastal zones. Ordinary Spanish citizens were strongly encouraged by successive governments to take out mortgages, even when repayment of loans was unlikely. Tax credits were granted to developers to build new holiday homes, towns and retirement settlements, often for wealthy pensioners coming from overseas in search of Spanish sun.

The growth rate of the construction industry was extraordinary (Charnock, Purcell & Ribera-Fumaz 2011) – it was so rapid and dependent on very high rates of interest, that when the global financial crisis (GFC) hit in 2007, many property developers went bankrupt within a matter of months. Unemployment, which was already high by European standards, rocketed. Regional governments, which had borrowed heavily on the national as well as international markets, struggled to repay their debts. A fiscal crisis at the regional and central state levels was the result. Public sector employment levels were cut, along with spending and investment cutbacks in health, education and social services. Spain became yet another laboratory for the International Monetary Fund (IMF) and the European Union's (EU's) austerity drive.

Spanish governments soon applied a strict policy of across-the-board cuts. The policy change began during the final stages of Prime Minister José Luis Rodríguez Zapatero's government (within the *Partido Socialista Obrero Español* [PSOE], the Spanish Socialist Workers' Party) and was later, in 2011, reinforced by Prime Minister Mariano Rajoy's government (*Partido Popular* [PP]). In May 2010, the Zapatero government altered its economic policy by cutting public expenditure in line with the austerity drive promoted by Germany and other EU member states. The austerity policy had two dimensions: cutting public expenditure and increasing state income through taxes and fees. In Spain, value-added tax (VAT) rates were raised twice (in 2011 and 2012), and personal income tax rates were also increased. Public expenditure was cut several times. Certain newly won citizen entitlements, such as the *cheque-bebé* (newborn baby allowance), were eliminated. Pensions were no longer adjusted for inflation; civil servants' pay was cut by 5 per cent. Unemployment rose so dramatically that by 2016, despite showing some signs of improvement, unemployment figures confirmed that there were still more than 3.7 million people unemployed and more than 1.55 million Spanish households with all members of working age out of work. Unemployment remained especially marked in the 20- to 24-year-old age group (43.3 per cent in June 2016). Budget cuts in the central and autonomous/local administrations were meanwhile enforced. A detailed report, *Cartografía de los recortes* (*Cartography of the Cuts*), was published in 2016 and confirmed that, during the period from early 2009 to late 2014, reductions in spending on education, health, unemployment and housing totalled €78.648 billion (Lago 2016). Paradoxically, during the same period, public debt soared from 52.7 per cent to 99.30 per cent of Spain's gross domestic product (GDP). The figure should not be surprising: During the same period, banks and savings companies received systematic financial support (García-Abadillo, Cebrián & Moreno 2015; Kickert & Ysa 2014).[1]

The economic crisis no doubt fed a deepening political crisis. As Spanish media began to probe the causes of the economic breakdown, the corruption of large parts of the political class was revealed. Media reports showed that the crisis was endemic in the sense that politicians of all parties and political persuasions, at every level of government, were deeply implicated. A doomsday scenario unfolded: defenders of electoral politics were faced with the decomposition of the political class as a whole.

It is against the backdrop of a crisis of the whole political economy that we need to understand the unfolding of events in 2011 and, in particular, the way in which the Arab uprisings in the early months of that year resonated among many citizens in Spain. Those uprisings, in Tunisia and elsewhere, showed that disaffiliated activists and those sickened by the spectacle of political parties and political elites could organise themselves to great effect. New media tools were used by activists to mobilise thousands of ordinary people; first, by organising demonstrations, and later by simply occupying public spaces in all of Spain's major cities and many towns and villages. The Arab uprisings and the Iceland protest in 2008 and 2009 served as examples and inspiration for an unprecedented popular mobilisation in Spain, now termed 15M because of the 15 May 2011 call-out (Castells 2012, pp. 115–120; Della Porta 2013).

In the political arena, the broad plurality of the forms of civil society participation emerging since 15M prompted some core questions. Which logics of participation – vertical or horizontal – predominate in this context of intense political engagement? What types of innovative political repertoires have taken root? And yet more relevant, how do the people involved analyse and interpret the appearance of these alternative forms of political participation? In an attempt to answer these questions, we begin by briefly describing some of the core notions surrounding the theoretical differentiation between vertical and horizontal logics of participation.

'Vertical' versus 'horizontal'

The distinction between 'vertical' and 'horizontal' political logics is a familiar theoretical axis used by scholars of social movements to reflect on heterogeneous political initiatives that may share the same goal (social transformation) but differ on how this goal could be, and must be, achieved (Robinson & Tormey 2005; Robinson & Tormey 2007; Juris 2005; Flesher Fominaya 2014a). These two positions diverge particularly in their approach to the representative structures and in their definitions of the most appropriate forms of political participation.

Vertical logic approaches follow the idea of building parties and 'taking' power. This form of politics is premised on the need for a programme setting out the party's policies and aims to convince and win over supporters. In turn, supporters will lend it sufficient social support with which to enter the structures of power and transform reality from inside. Its aim is to win power so as to establish, from above, its vision and model of society and politics. This vertical logic of political practice holds 'an image of power as a macrosocial resource which one can possess' (Robinson & Tormey 2007, p. 128). It assumes that there is a 'centre' of power that can be occupied and, once taken over, gives power holders the opportunity to mould society according to the principles they defend. Intrinsic to this perspective is the notion that there is no other way 'outside' representation and representative politics. All politics has some level of representation; the sooner civil society embraces this conception the sooner it will be in a position to effectively oppose the political and economic elites. Political thinkers who defend this type of participation include Žižek (2010) among others.

In contrast, horizontal logics approaches advocate creating alternative spaces where people can interact to mutual benefit. Defenders of horizontal logics seek to undermine the hegemony of existing political forces while stimulating alternative social, economic and political relationships. In other words, they promote 'an activist rhizomatics, a way in which networks can coalesce, develop, multiply and re-multiply' (Robinson & Tormey 2005). Advocates of horizontal logics regard programmes and political parties as unnecessary. What is needed are spaces for gathering, shared learning and solidarity – support networks that can unite to mobilise and put pressure on the logics of the system. The kinds of interaction underlying these relationships eschew hierarchy, formal organisation and bureaucracy. It is the spread of alternative practices that will lead to political transformation (Tormey 2015a). Among the authors writing on this theoretical framework are Holloway (2002) and Graeber (2013).

By differentiating between the theories of ideal types of political logics, we are able to observe their corresponding political repertoires. Actions typical of the vertical model include drawing up manifestos and programmes, taking part in strikes, proposing legal reforms and constituting political parties. The horizontal model, in contrast, implements strategies such as demonstrations and acts of civil disobedience and promotes forms of group self-organisation. The two ways of doing politics also differ in their position on political institutions. The vertical model advocates mobilisations designed to negotiate, influence or pressurise these institutions; the horizontal model follows the option of contention, rejecting the notion that central political institutions can bring about social transformation.

Debate and reflection on the desirability of one particular logic of participation over another is not confined to theory but is also the origin of much discussion among civil society activists and actors. This is the case in the 15M movement and all its forms of political expression: demonstrations, occupations, setting up political parties and so on. Because of the plurality of actors and forms of political participation involved, it is unadvisable to make simplistic associations on this point. To help clarify this complex issue we now introduce some of the most innovative political repertoires that have taken root since 2011.

Towards a differentiation of the 15M political repertoire

The transversal, changing and plural nature of 15M makes it difficult to provide categorical explanations of the movement and its component parts. Any approach aiming to differentiate types of participation within the wide political repertoire of this movement should be made with caution. There is no doubt, however, that the 15M movement has ushered in an original and creative political repertoire that, since 2011, has altered the role citizens play in politics and has changed the channels and methods used for political transformation (Feenstra 2015). This repertoire has two basic defining elements: 1) participants' use of the potential offered by digital and analogue spaces; and 2) evolution of the political repertoire in line with the context and collective learning.

In the various forms of participation that we will describe in this chapter, there is a close link between online and offline forms of participation. In defining the political repertoire, we take into account the chronology of events and differences in the movement's stages, focusing on changes in citizen participation arising from collective learning. Specifically, we analyse: 1) call-outs and demonstrations without the traditional intermediary structures; 2) *acampadas* and assemblies; 3) the formulation and dissemination of ideas, as well as coordination and modification of media and political agendas, through digital tools; 4) citizen monitoring processes and platforms; 5) stopping evictions; 6) popular legislative initiatives and *escraches*; 7) citizen *mareas* (protest movements; literally, 'tides') against social spending cuts; 8) sieges of representative institutions (e.g. surrounding parliament); 9) blockades and occupations of institutions and megaprojects; and 10) the emergence of new political parties.

Call-outs and demonstrations without the traditional intermediary
structures (trade unions and political parties)

On 15 May 2011 (hence the movement's name, 15M), the first
demonstration began under the slogan 'We aren't merchandise in politicians' and bankers' hands' (Monterde et al. 2015). Expressions of
outrage spread quickly through many Spanish cities. What was most
innovative in the organisation of this outbreak of public protest was
that none of the traditional political structures was involved (Della
Porta 2013; Subirats 2011). Trade unions and political parties were
notable by their absence in the call-out and the organisation of 15M, a
circumstance that triggered a creative explosion of messages, symbols
and demands (Castells 2012). Digital networks played a vital role in
organising, mobilising and publicising 15M (Postill 2014; Anduiza,
Cristancho & Sabucedo 2014; Toret 2013). In turn, the traditional
mass media's role of spreading information about the movement was
marginal at the beginning. The proliferation of demonstrations, the
acampadas and the mass dissemination through social networks eventually prompted increasingly widespread coverage of the protests in the
mainstream media (Micó & Casero-Ripollés 2014). In this initial phase
of the movement, expressions of anger took the form of general criti-
cisms of deficiencies in the political system and demands for 'more
democracy' and 'real democracy'. On 15 October, the first international *indignados* call-out resulted in actions in 1051 cities in 90 countries. Shortly before that, on 17 September, Occupy Wall Street had
begun in the United States.

'Acampadas' and assemblies

A few hours after the demonstrations started on 15 May, suggestions
were made to continue the street protests with permanent occupations
in the public squares. Images of the revolts in Arab countries resonated
with Spanish activists, who quickly decided to take back public spaces
by organising *acampadas* (occupations) in over 55 cities (Flesher
Fominaya 2014a; Romanos 2013; Tejerina & Perugorría 2012; Benski
et al. 2013). The most striking feature of these *acampadas* was the
assembly decision-making model. Each *acampada* had two key structures: the general assembly for adopting collective decisions, and the
committees (e.g. action, communication, IT, legal and infrastructure)
so participants could engage with the areas they were most interested
in. Although the committees required some specialist knowledge or
skills, all key decisions and political proposals were debated in the

general assembly. The aim of these assemblies was to reach a consensus on a minimum agenda. At this stage the dynamics of participation were seen as equally important as, or perhaps even more important than, the results in themselves.

Formulation and dissemination of ideas and coordination and modification of the media and political agendas through digital tools

Coinciding with the *acampadas*, new communication tools were being used not only as mechanisms for call-outs and promoting online petitions (or votes) but also to develop and disseminate the ideas and proposals coming out of the *acampadas*. Network collaboration processes increased the pressure on the mainstream media to include new issues on both traditional and alternative media agendas (Casero-Ripollés & Feenstra 2012). These online dynamics strengthened other mechanisms put into action in the *acampadas* and would continue once the occupations were dismantled. They will be discussed in greater depth in Chapter 4.

Citizen monitoring processes and platforms

Shortly after the start of 15M, platforms began to appear that would monitor and scrutinise centres of political and economic power in Spain. An explosion of initiatives were spawned specialising in tracking politicians' actions, extracting hidden information, drawing up reports, sharing information in open formats and the like. These platforms made efficient use of digital tools in their investigations into cases of possible abuse of power and corruption, which they subsequently made public. Alongside these platforms, citizens also banded together in initiatives for collaborative scrutiny that exploited the potential of new communication tools to uncover possible abuses of power or specific malpractices. An exemplary case of such an initiative is 15MpaRato (Tascón & Quintana 2012). Specialised denouncing and monitoring processes took shape as a new political dynamic (Feenstra & Keane 2014) and is examined in more detail in Chapter 3.

Stopping evictions

One of the most significant political expressions in the context of the economic crisis is the prevention of evictions. Since its creation, the *Plataforma de Afectados por la Hipoteca* (PAH; Platforms of People Affected by Mortgages) has prevented more than 2045 evictions[2] using tactics in which activists act as human shields to physically stop the police and bailiffs from entering, thereby preventing their occupants from being evicted. The PAH is one of the most renowned groups with links to 15M. It predates the 15M, although there is a strong symbiosis between the two movements, and the PAH continued to grow steadily as a result of the emergence of 15M in 2011. The PAH is now a broad network of platforms present in more than 145 cities. It was founded in 2009 as part of a broader social movement that had been campaigning for access to decent housing since 2003 (Romanos 2013). The PAH was set up to protest against mortgage abuses and to alleviate the problems of finding housing in a period of crisis. Over the years it has raised public awareness of abusive clauses in mortgage agreements and has placed the question of assets in lieu of payment firmly on the media agenda.

Popular legislative initiatives and 'escraches'

Another form of participation the PAH uses is the popular legislative initiative (PLI). It initiated a PLI to propose a reform of the mortgage law. After many complications, the law eventually came before parliament in 2003 having obtained more than 1.4 million signatures. This initiative called for a specific legislative proposal to be drawn up to replace the current legislation. Before it could be debated in parliament, the proposal had to be disseminated widely and required a large number of citizen signatures. Former PAH spokesperson Ada Colau was a member of the parliamentary committee set up in 2013 to draft the law reform proposal. This political initiative reflected the PAH's decision to explore the possibility of political transformation through representative institutions. The Spanish government, however, radically altered the draft on its passage through the parliamentary machine.

Coinciding with this initiative, the PAH stepped up pressure on politicians through what are known as *escraches*, demonstrations outside politicians' homes.[3] Those targeted were the politicians responsible for deciding whether to proceed with the popular legislative initiative.[4] The PAH began using this strategy in March 2013 as a way of pressurising politicians to ensure their demands were heard and to form a collective negotiation process (Romanos 2014).

Citizen 'mareas' against social spending cuts

Citizen *mareas*, or public protests, against public spending cuts and in defence of essential public services began in 2012. These *mareas* were identified by colours associated with their fields of action – for example, *Marea Blanca* (white for the health service), *Marea Verde* (green for education), *Marea Granate* (maroon for forced migration) and the like. This hybrid movement is innovative in the way it brings together traditional structures and new dynamics. Traditional trade union tactics are adopted, but the *mareas* are more self-organised, inclusive, distributed and horizontal in their actions. This structure has attracted participants from a wide range of backgrounds including experts, service users, professionals and activists. Its biggest success was achieved by the Madrid *Marea Blanca* which, in 2013 and 2014, uncovered corruption in the attempt to privatise numerous hospitals in the region and brought the process to a halt. Demonstrations, reports, assemblies and negotiation with representatives form part of the *mareas'* repertoire of strategies.

Siege of representative institutions (e.g. surrounding parliament), blockades and occupations of institutions and megaprojects

Towards the end of 2012, demonstrations began to take on a new form. On 25 September in Madrid, the *Plataforma ¡En Pie!* and *Coordinadora 25-S* organised the 'Surround Parliament' (also known as 25-S, and initially as Occupy Parliament). This action consists of symbolically besieging representative institutions and focuses protests on specific places or institutions. Other citizens follow the events streamed on the internet or through messages posted on channels like Twitter. The aim of this type of protest is to single out those deemed to be responsible for causing political and social unrest.

Another form of political action used successfully in recent years is to occupy or blockade institutions or large urban projects in order to disrupt their normal day-to-day operations for the purpose of publicly denouncing malpractice or injustice. Such actions have spread to banks and town or city halls with the involvement of groups such as *iai@flautas* (older protesters or 'old hippies') and PAH. One of the most high-profile campaigns was *Toque a Bankia* (Pulling up Bankia) in May 2013. Protests were held outside Bankia bank branches all over Spain in protest against the cash injection from public funds the bank received – €18 billion. One of the most prominent blockades of a megaproject was the 'Gamonal case', which started with neighbourhood protests against the construction, at a cost of €8 million, of a boulevard in an economically depressed area of Burgos (in northern Spain). The local community regarded this as a waste of public money in an area of the city that lacked decent coverage of some public services. Other projects regarded as unnecessary have been stopped elsewhere in the country, such as the demolition of the *Can Vives* squat in Barcelona.

The emergence of new political parties

A more recent trend, and perhaps one of the most striking, is the appearance of new political parties founded by people with a history of grassroots activism. Since 2011, a steady stream of new parties has emerged, some of the most relevant being *Partido X* (2013) and *Podemos* (2014) and various city-based platforms (e.g. *Barcelona en Común, Ahora Madrid, Zaragoza en Común* and *Castellón en Moviment*, to name just a few that were created between 2014 and 2015). These groups differ from traditional parties in that, as well as incorporating new political demands, they also integrate new dynamics (e.g. transparency and participation) into their own organisational structures. These initiatives understand the political party is just one of many tools for political participation. Digital channels are also essential to these parties' internal organisation and growth and for spreading information about their proposals. After many years of grassroots activism, these new political groups now form part of the electoral landscape, bringing with them the demands of 15M which they now attempt to defend from within the representative institutions.

The 15M political repertoire and the vertical–horizontal theoretical axis

The plurality and evolution in the forms of participation emerging from 15M raise some interesting points for political reflection about the movement. The way they combine elements from the repertoires identified in the vertical–horizontal theoretical axis is particularly interesting and calls into question the usefulness of this differentiation to understand activism in the Spanish context. The importance and repercussions of the *acampadas* and assemblies, at both national and international levels, might *a priori* suggest a clear predominance of the horizontal logic of citizen participation. While these horizontal forms of political expression did indeed hold sway in the early days of the 15M, analysis of the political repertoire that has unfolded since then reveals the complexity of this issue. At the same time, the recent proliferation of new political parties, with grassroots activists linked to 15M, suggests a shift towards political institutionalisation and, therefore, towards a more vertical model. The political repertoire described above uncovers some interesting combinations, or hybridisation, of vertical and horizontal forms of participation, as we shall see from the following analysis.

As different and more innovative ways of participating developed, several single-issue platforms seeking solutions to specific problems began to take shape. One illustration is the mortgage law issue which was addressed in a popular legislative initiative and by pressurising and negotiating with representative institutions. This case fits into the vertical model – keeping to the rules of the democratic game to bring about political change through parliament. This political action, pursued through 'traditional' channels and backed by over 1.4 million signatures, was also accompanied by direct action in the form of bank occupations and *escraches* – acts of civil disobedience. This kind of participation is grounded in pressure, non-violence and the defence of universal rights, practices which all come very close to the limits of legality and in which participants assume the risk of arrest and prosecution (Habermas 1998; García Marzá 1998). This example illustrates how a platform such as PAH takes elements from both vertical and horizontal logics to strengthen its political demands and achieves political change (Ordóñez, Feenstra & Tormey 2015). The citizen *mareas* also combine elements from horizontal and vertical models. They follow traditional trade union models that are close to the representative structures to deal with the public bureaucratic system, in line with the vertical logic. Yet they also incorporate the new culture and codes from 15M, in the form of open assemblies, in which professionals, affected parties, parents, students and others can all engage. These are institutionalised platforms that draw up manifestos and aspire to negotiate with representative structures. At the same time, they are also openly inclusive and distributed spaces for self-organisation.

Finally, we turn to what is perhaps the most novel aspect of the proliferation of new political parties created by grassroots activists. In the last few years, the phenomenon of new or reconstituted political parties has been a constant element in the Spanish political landscape, coinciding with the decline in popularity of the traditional parties. These new parties, such as *Podemos*, *Partido X* and various municipal council platforms, were largely founded by activists who, having considered alternative external channels of protest and pressure, switched strategies to stand for election. In effect, they have taken the step into institutionalised politics with all its structures, programmes and internal rules. By following the steps of vertical logic, they are accepting that representation is unavoidable as a way of transforming political reality (Tormey 2015a). These new parties, however, build horizontal elements into their own structures to prevent elite groups from forming, and they remain open to civil society and grassroots activists, thereby supporting the incorporation of assemblies and other horizontal elements into their internal operations and decision-making processes. These parties now face the challenge of balancing the horizontal–vertical combination and keeping their connections with civil society alive and healthy.

In summary, 15M opened up the way for a repertoire of complex, dynamic actions in which horizontal and vertical elements are creatively combined. The movement's initial phase of occupying public spaces also reflected its interest in forms of political participation akin to horizontal models; however, as the political repertoire evolved, its focus on specific demands and actions grew. Over time, some elements from the vertical model have gained sway in terms of institutionalising political practices, but without abandoning aspects from the horizontal logics previously experimented with. At this juncture, the question arises of whether the tension between the combined vertical and horizontal elements is acknowledged by the actors involved in the forms of political action described here. What do the activists have to say about the forms of participation they are promoting?

Activists' responses to the vertical–horizontal axis

One core aspect of the current political situation is that at least some of the basic premises of political strategies, both vertical and horizontal, are being called into question. The proponents of the strategy of the horizontal logic, based on fostering autonomous initiatives and alternative lifestyles against the representative structures, clashes with the reality marked by the internationalisation of the economy and by complex mechanisms of 'multilevel' governance. While horizontal initiatives might proliferate in Spain in the short-term future, it seems unlikely that this process will, by itself, trigger the radical transformation of the political system or seriously jeopardise the elites' tenacious hold on their positions of power. Defenders of the 'vertical' logic also face a variety of difficulties. The electoral system has its own limitations that affect access to power through the representative structures, particularly for smaller and non-mainstream parties. Other hurdles that social movements face along the vertical route include problems of access to the financial resources enjoyed by the traditional parties, difficulties in extending their influence through the mainstream media and concern that they will be swallowed up by the 'networks of the system'. We now turn to some of the most significant and widespread responses from the activists themselves on these and other issues.

Towards a purely assembly-based model?

Before carrying out our interviews, the huge international following the *acampadas* had attracted suggested there would be a preference for horizontal forms of political participation; however, our meetings with the activists soon dispelled any such preconceptions. The main vehicle for autonomous initiatives is the assembly, which sprang up in most Spanish cities and towns with 15M (Castañeda 2012; Castells 2012). These initiatives followed a deliberative model designed to reach consensus on developing platforms, manifestos and specific demands, following the type of dynamics familiar to observers of Zapatista initiatives (Holloway 2002; Tormey 2006). The limitations of this model soon became evident to those who had participated in 15M (Castells 2012). The combination of the desire for consensus with open deliberation leaves the decision-making process vulnerable to sabotage by small groups; in practice, therefore, this model presented certain specific problems.

In our meetings with assembly participants, we heard several complaints about difficulties in reaching agreements. Some members of the action committee in Valencia criticised the objections raised by more cautious activists and the countless obstacles to their action proposals from members of the legal committee. As for the general assembly, some activists were critical of the way 'hours could often go by without any consensus being reached. After a while, this would get very exhausting' (Activist 1, Barcelona). Others said that, due to lack of time, 'only students or young activists were able to follow these lengthy decision-making processes through to the end' (Activist 1, Castellón). Another criticism was the 'presence of trolls whose only purpose was to block any kind of agreement or consensus' (Activist 2, Barcelona). It became clear from these conversations with the activists that decision-making was time consuming, laborious and demoralising when even simple decisions could be blocked by a handful of individuals exercising power of veto.

Despite the assembly model's limitations, the activists acknowledged the experience as an essential part of their political development and their understanding of politics. Twelve of the interviewees described participation in the assembly process as a 'vital experience' in their political preparation. Some were quick to define the assemblies as 'the best university for learning how to share different points of view' (Activist 3, Barcelona) and 'the best antidote to any kind of dogmatism' (Activist 1, Valencia). The long, exhausting hours of debate in the city squares taught them that 'politics is complex and it requires patience' (Activist 2, Valencia).

Despite recognising the assemblies as essential to the political and collective learning process, the general conclusion the activists drew was, as a form of political expression, assemblies were not enough to bring about political transformation. They favoured complementing, extending and experimenting with other forms of participation, particularly the following three options: 1) the 'technological solution' of transferring the decision-making task to the virtual sphere through new communication technologies; 2) sacrificing the medium- and long-term horizons to concentrate on short-term goals, particularly issues that could be resolved to immediate and measurable effect; and 3) participation through the polls.

Given the critical role of digital tools in the emergence and mobilisation of 15M, it was no surprise to learn that the activists had full confidence in such mechanisms to overcome some of the shortcomings of the assembly format. The idea behind this conviction is that open and inclusive technology could promote a consensual decision-making process valid not only for mobilisation but also for questions of governance. The general perception is that new technology can be used to smooth the way towards a form of decision making that avoids the tedious dynamics of the assembly while at the same time extending channels of participation beyond the cyclical elections of the strictly representative system.

Many activists expressed a desire to become directly involved in issues and actions that impact normal people's lives. Perhaps the most obvious examples of this are the PAH and the *iai@flautas*. The PAH's numerous direct and immediate actions include stopping evictions, providing advice for citizens affected by mortgages and providing information on abusive clauses in mortgage agreements, and campaigning for changes in mortgage legislation. The *iai@flautas*, who define themselves as children of the 15M, defend the need for immediate non-ideological activism aimed at protecting the welfare state and putting an end to the excesses perpetrated by politicians and parties of every hue. Both groups advocate direct action to pursue immediate changes to specific problems. The members of both groups expressed great disaffection with the large political parties and, although they agreed that the 'political class' badly needed a major overhaul, their inclinations were more towards taking direct action against 'specific acts of injustice and cuts in social issues' (*iai@flauta* 1, Barcelona). One activist expressed this clearly, saying that 'citizens are suffering and there is no time to be lost. We must put a stop to evictions, change the mortgage law and call for social support for people with financial problems' (PAH activist 1, Castellón). Members of both groups showed a clear preference for a type of political activism that 'perhaps might not be enough to change the system completely, but can achieve small victories' (PAH activist 2, Barcelona).

Our interviews also revealed proposals for a third type of participation as an alternative to, or in conjunction with, the assemblies: new political parties. This option was voiced particularly by the younger activists interviewed and was a position that evolved and grew notably between 2012 and 2014. In 2012, while only a few people were open to the idea of 'competing in the electoral arena' (Activist 3, Barcelona), in the following years many others began to claim that 'challenges must be made to the power in numerous spaces, but especially where it hurts them most, in the representative institutions' (Activist 3, Valencia). Formations such as *Partido X, Podemos* and *Barcelona en Común* began to appear as basic mechanisms for achieving political transformation. These will be analysed in Chapter 2.

No to politicians, but yes to other leadership models

Another pertinent issue when considering possible avenues and strategies for political transformation is the potential role of a charismatic leader in this process. What is the value of a leader in the political transformation process? In our interviews and discussions with activists, we met with little enthusiasm for the idea of a charismatic leader as a unifier of wide-ranging sensibilities, capable of guiding and providing the necessary inspiration to achieve change (Laclau 1996; Žižek 2001; Dean 2009). The leader as indispensable to processes of political change was generally viewed with scepticism. The Spanish context is an example of the patent failure of politicians of all political stripes to demonstrate the type of leadership that can assuage fears of nepotism and corruption. Few were attracted by a model of political transformation led by an individual or group of people like those at the helm in the country. The importance of a model of *exemplary leadership*, though, was clearly recognised: someone who through their own actions reflects the values and interests shared by those around them.

A good illustration of such exemplary leadership in action is Ada Colau, who gained a high public profile as the spokesperson of the PAH. At the time of our meetings with activists in 2013, Colau's face was all over the media, on television, in the newspapers and on social media. Many of the activists interviewed regarded her as 'a leader', but a leader in the sense that she was able to articulate, in direct and emotive terms, what many other activists in and beyond the PAH saw as key issues. These issues included the injustice of evictions, the government's lack of response to the needs and interests of ordinary people, and the greed of the political and economic elites. Some notable comments about her were that 'Ada brings to light the problems that affect the Spanish people. It's because of her that the platform's demands have gained strength' (PAH activist 2, Barcelona). Others praised her ability 'to stand up to the politicians in parliament and tell them that the Spanish mortgage law is a scam' (*iai@flauta* 3, Barcelona). Similarly, at 15Mp2p, a meeting of academics held at the Open University of Catalonia on 5 July 2012, PAH activist Gala Pin, referring to Ada Colau, stated:

> [T]he context needs a face, and there is also an impulse or a demand from the media, and when the question comes up of sharing out PAH spokesperson tasks […] there is a widespread call to keep this face because, in effect, she represents what the movement defends […] and she serves in this role to make the platform visible.[5]

Colau is regarded as just another member of the platform, close to the movement's bases, and she is appreciated as a leader of citizens and not just another politician.

In 2014, references to another figure in this line of exemplary leadership began to be heard in the conversations with civil society activists: that of Pablo Iglesias. Those we interviewed saw him as 'capable of putting into words the indignation many citizens feel' (*Podemos* member 2, Valencia) or as an 'intelligent person with the ability to stand up to the political elites' (*Podemos* member 3, Barcelona).

Both figures, now leading the political projects of *Barcelona en Común* and *Podemos*, respectively, are facing the challenge of how to remain close to civil society and continue to be seen as approachable representatives of activists' demands. Whether or not they can maintain the image of an exemplary leader, as opposed to the standard political leader, will depend on their ability to forge an alternative model of leadership.

Is the party over?

Activists sympathetic to the idea of building a political party identify various obstacles, the most obvious of which is the distance from, and even animosity towards, political representatives – in general, the whole political class. Political representatives are seen as marked by corruption and the desire to line their own pockets instead of dealing with the country's problems. From this perspective, politics through the representative structures is seen as aloof and distant from society. Political parties are regarded as vehicles for personal opportunism, a means for those with ambitions of power and wealth to achieve their goals. The idea of a political party as a potential vehicle for political transformation and for achieving a better, or 'real', democracy, *a priori* sounds somewhat contradictory.

However, the activists' stance on the possibility of participating or influencing things through the electoral process should not in any way be ignored; although rejection of the traditional political parties is palpable, since 2013 there has also been a noticeable shift in favour of the party option, accompanied by a steady stream of new political parties. This does not mean they are seeking to replicate the traditional party dynamics. What is unusual about these new parties is precisely their alternative understanding of how this type of organisation works. For this reason, parties may arise as a way to highlight the limitations affecting the traditional parties, as a means of protest against the political class or as a mechanism to take politics from the street into parliament. We explore this trend in the formation of new parties in greater detail in the following chapter.

Parties are seen as strategic tools with which to open up new channels of participation and influence in the political system. Obviously there are significant subtle differences among these new parties, but all of them seek to set themselves apart from the traditional vertical model of participation. These parties aim to incorporate horizontal mechanisms that will encourage civil society participation and reduce the distance between representatives and represented. As we shall see later in the book, this is precisely the challenge that defines the *raison d'être* of many of these initiatives.

Towards a characterisation of 15M

Defining and detailing the shared characteristics of participants in a movement as plural and complex as 15M is no easy task. Although we do not set out to present any definite conclusions on the nature of the participant actors and their dynamics, we did identify some repeated patterns in the conversations and interviews conducted between 2013 and 2015. Two basic aspects stand out: 1) defence of the need for a pragmatic approach to procedures and political strategies; and 2) willingness to leave behind preconceptions in favour of a plural approach based on experimentation and creativity. These two aspects influence the activists by undermining any sense of certainty about what the right strategy is. They also have the effect of creating a radically contingent space for deliberation and debate on the best way forward. But how is this articulated in relation to the vertical–horizontal axis?

During this research it was particularly striking just how willing activists were to think creatively in reaching decisions on the strategies, tactics and vehicles with which to express political opposition. Those we interviewed showed a high level of awareness of the difference between theorising about political transformation and applying it in practice in far from ideal circumstances. The theoretical axis that differentiates the horizontal from the vertical levels of doing politics, a familiar tool in activists' and academics' repertoires, seems strangely inadequate to capture and explain the movement's objectives or dynamics, at least if we regard the two extremes as opposing logics. Practically every group and every individual activist appeared to incorporate aspects of both the horizontal and the vertical models into their own reflections and practices as participating actors.

Linked to this question is the notable absence of any class ideology. This 'lack' is not because the activists had no interest in the class question, but rather because of a determined position not to present any set of pre-established ideas about what a society should be like or how it should function. Concerns focused instead on the process – on how to improve the quality of democratic processes. This radicalism was driven by a rejection of the existing situation and by disillusionment and discontent with the status quo. It is not based on a positioning that pursues a rigorous theoretical or normative definition of an alternative world. The activists know what they do not like, but they are less sure about what they support. Far from this being an impediment to political action, and contrary to what authors such as Žižek (2001; 2010) and others argue, it is precisely this lack of certainty that has provided the grounds on which to consolidate the forms and style of political interaction characteristic of 15M since its inception. In the absence of an absolute political 'truth' that dispenses with any need for debate and dialogue, these activists consider that a dialogical process must avoid the great and given truths or certainties in order to listen to and participate with other activists. It is precisely the lack of a concrete *telos* which provided – and still provides – the base on which to establish the process of interactive deliberation, the opposite of a deductive process that shows and marks 'the way'.

Conclusions

The certainties that buoyed previous generations of activists seem notable by their absence in our research. None of the activists we interviewed claimed to have a firm idea about the specific 'right' way Spain should address its current crisis, nor did anyone reveal a preferred formula for creating a better society. There was a notable absence of any solid normative framework. Indeed, when asked which strategy they thought activists should follow to achieve political transformation and real democracy, the most common response we heard was 'I don't know'. They seemed to view the future as deeply uncertain, contingent and therefore open. It was of course this latter point that gave them hope that their interventions might make a difference to the current situation, perhaps not today or tomorrow, but maybe the day after, or the day after that. They were, as Lyotard (1984) puts it, 'pagans' whose activism is sustained not by knowledge of the hereafter, but by the simple opposition to injustice, inequality and an antiquated political system. Of course for Žižek (2010), Badiou (1989) and other authors, such a stance is doomed to failure; without certainty, without a 'truth', political energies dissipate. And this may well be the case, but there are examples in the history of social transformation that paint the opposite picture. It was injustice that inspired anti-colonial movements, civil rights movements, movements against discrimination and exploitation, and many more. Like those involved in the 15M, the activists in these movements knew less about what they wanted to build, but they knew full well what they were against. Most important of all, they won their battles.

What we can learn from our analysis of how the 15M political repertoire has evolved, and from its actors' viewpoints, is that their pragmatic and open thinking has firmed up a constantly evolving and reconfiguring political context. In this landscape, the strict theoretical divisions between horizontal and vertical logics lose importance – it is in the hybridisation of the two that its dynamics can best be contextualised. This non-dogmatic, reflective position strengthens the view of the Spanish context as a political laboratory where different elements and repertoires are constantly combining. The activists' pursuit of 'real democracy' demands the constant rethinking of different ways or strategies to achieve it. Particularly since 2014, it is the strengthened commitment to new political parties with which to enter institutional channels. This new landscape is also part of 15M activists' search for new formats and experimentation and is the subject we explore in the next chapter.

Notes

1 The Spanish Securities and Investment Board (CNMC) estimated that between 2008 and 2013, the financial sector received €94.753 billion in aid. This figure includes substantial resources invested in recapitalising financial

institutions (€61.853 billion) and the salvaging of damaged assets (€32.9 billion).

2 Information verified on 15 September 2016. Source: http://afectadosporlahip oteca.com/.

3 A form of political action used by human rights groups to denounce the impunity of those responsible for *los desaparecidos* (the disappeared). The expression originated in Argentina in the 1990s; see John Keane (2009), pp. 786–787.

4 The legality of this method was questioned because it took place outside politicians' homes. It is, however, considered as an act of civil disobedience (nonviolent and with prior notification) aimed at raising politicians' awareness of the way certain human rights are ignored. A high-profile *escrache* was held outside the house of the vice president, Soraya Sáenz de Santamaria (5 April 2013). Despite complaints from renowned government politicians, Madrid's Court number 4 considered the *escrache* a 'legal mechanism of democratic participation' and an 'expression of citizens' pluralism' (our translation). See the sentence at: http://ep00.epimg.net/desca rgables/2013/05/10/cb072919fb0bac890565b82873b2f89e.pdf.

Several months later a judge in Section 16 of the Madrid Provincial Court ratified this sentence. See: http://ep00.epimg.net/descargables/2014/02/04/9036e637be04ef9e3242f1fd78fc0c84.pdf.

5 Gala Pin's observations (in Spanish) on Ada Colau from the 15MP2P meeting are available at: http://bambuser.com/v/3715363 (Minutes 58:30–62:00).

2   The emergence of new political parties

Since 2008, when the economic crisis unleashed by the global financial collapse hit Spain, the number of new political parties has rocketed. Between 2009 and 2010, the Spanish Ministry of Internal Affairs registered 295 new political parties. In the period of protests and mobilisations between 2011 and 2012, this figure nearly doubled to 492. The number rose again in the period between 1 January 2014 and 20 April 2015, with a further 522 new parties registered (368 of which were formed in the first months of 2015).[1] While most of these newly registered parties had no political impact at a national level, there was a notable appearance and presence of parties promoting, to some extent, transformation of the coordinates of the political system. These initiatives included some parties who were associated with 15M (e.g. *Podemos* and *Partido X* as well as the numerous municipal council initiatives inspired by *Barcelona en Común* [2]) because they had members in common and shared some demands. Others, such as the *Partido Pirata* (Pirate Party) or *Escaños en Blanco* (Blank Seats), put forward innovative proposals. At one level, these developments should be welcomed by those who view a healthy and vibrant range of parties as an essential part of representative democracy; however, they have also thrown up many conundrums that need to be solved.

First, how can this explosion of political parties be explained, bearing in mind the picture of party decline over the past decade? (Dalton 2004; Lawson 2010; Whiteley 2011; van Biezen, Mair & Poguntke 2012). If political parties are in decline, what is behind the sudden preference for the party format among Spain's politically active citizens? (Diani & McAdam 2003; Castells 2012).

Second, it is well documented (Castells 2012) that the 15M mobilisations were initially characterised by highly participatory occupations, street protests and assemblies involving between 6.5 and 8 million citizens according to some estimates (FnfEurope 2013). Given this extraordinary level of engagement, seemingly based on a rejection of political parties and the system of representation in its entirety (Hughes 2011), how is it that the mobilisations appear to have given increased impetus to this mushrooming of new political parties?

Third, what does this proliferation of parties tell us, more broadly, about the future of 'party-based democracy' in Spain and elsewhere? Can this proliferation be explained by its support for the party-based democracy typical of the Western political system, or are we seeing an important change in the relationships among citizens, parties and governance?

From street protests to taking over the institutions

Based on our research, the key drivers for the proliferation of new parties are as follows: 1) the context of political and economic crisis in Spain that has engulfed the political class as a whole, in particular the two main political parties, the PSOE and the PP; 2) the dramatic fall in the costs of setting up a party as a result of advances in digital media technologies; and 3) the perceived limitation of 'grassroots politics', direct action and other kinds of direct and indirect lobbying in leveraging change in the politics and agenda of the traditional parties.

This has meant that even the staunchest supporters of horizontal activism – such as assemblies, demonstrations and occupations – have begun to view the party format as a possible tool for political change that does not necessarily compromise the ideals of street-based activism. The result is that the new parties depart significantly from the traditional political parties. In turn this impacts upon both the meaning of party-based democracy and the connotations of the term 'participation' going beyond the boundaries of civil society.

As noted in the previous chapter, it seems evident that most, although not all, of the activists concluded that any advance towards political reforms and changes can occur only if they participate in the electoral process. Given the limited scope of the street protests and the huge amounts of energy demanded by the *acampadas* and assemblies, a more permanent way was sought to keep up pressure on the political elites. It is here that the enthusiasm for political parties has its roots. This situation can be understood by looking at the different types of parties set up since 2011, many of which emerged as a result of the motivations described below.

1) As a mechanism of protest against the political class

15M was directly inspired by the desire to change the mindset or behaviour of political elites (Castells 2012; Della Porta 2013). Because the assemblies were only partially successful in achieving this goal, more direct means were needed to make the point. With this in mind, the focus of *Podemos's* European election campaign in 2014 was to constantly criticise the political elites and, more specifically, *la casta* (the political class). The base of *Podemos*'s political message reflects the binary nature of the opposition of elites and citizens. Referring to the creation of the party, Iñigo Errejón says, 'In Spain we saw that on the one hand, we had the political caste, and on the other, the citizens'.[3] *Podemos* members echo this idea, arguing that their initiative 'is more than a left-wing party; it is a party of protest against the caste' (*Podemos* member 1), or 'up to now political participation has belonged to the elites, but this is no longer the case. Citizens have a voice in this movement/party' (*Podemos* member 2). This anti-elite factor is equally important in the case of *Barcelona en Común*, a political project initiated early in 2014 to contest the 2015 local elections in Barcelona, which provided a platform for groups associated with 15M to come together politically. Its pillars are to stimulate new practices and to build a project based on strict ethical criteria. On these conditions, *Barcelona en Común* is open to alliances with all parties except, according to Ada Colau, 'the parties of the regime that are directly responsible not only for governing the city, but the country as a whole'. The parties 'of the regime' – the political elites – include 'PP, PSOE and CiU' (i.e. Convergence and Union, Catalonia).[4]

Similarly, *Escaños en Blanco* (EB), which won 115,308 votes in the 2014 European elections, was created in 2010 to highlight disillusionment with the existing political class.[5] The party would 'run candidates who promised not to take up their seats in regional or national parliaments if they were elected' (*EB* member 1). This would leave a 'blank' or empty seat in the representative institutions, serving as a reminder of the electorate's anger and disillusionment with their representatives. Apart from this simple idea, *Escaños en Blanco* does not have a programme as such. Its manifesto has but one single point: 'to leave the seat empty'.[6] *Escaños en Blanco* offers no solutions to the wider economic, political and social crises. It sees itself as an organisation with a single goal: 'to make visible citizens' dissatisfaction and leave no doubt about their feeling that politicians do not represent them properly' (*EB* member 2). This means that the organisation can present itself as non-ideological and 'above the fray'. It also means that its internal organisation is simple and relatively non-hierarchical. Because it has no programme to debate, it can 'concentrate on strategic and tactical issues' (*EB* member 3).

2) As a mechanism for bringing the 'street' directly into politics

An interesting facet of the current political situation in Spain is the willingness of activists to use the party format as a vehicle for mobilisation and a strategy to highlight the limitations of the present political system. One example is *Partido X*, founded at the beginning of 2013 by members of 15M. In the words of one activist, it was set up to 'get the politicians out of the institutions and put decision making back in the hands of the people' (*Partido X* member 1), with the goal of fostering a 'true democracy where citizens have a voice and can control the decision-making process' (*Partido X* member 2). This is a decentralised model of democracy known as *democracia y punto* (democracy, full stop).[7] As one *Partido X* member put it, 'now that it's possible with ICTs, it's time to introduce new forms of government that recognise society's ability to directly improve its own institutions and laws' (*Partido X* member 3).

When *Podemos* was founded in 2014, it brought in some of the dynamics from 15M, particularly regarding territorial organisation. Participation grew through assemblies, known as *círculos*, or circles, meeting in public spaces across Spain and abroad. During the first half of 2014, more than 400 circles sprang up in neighbourhoods, villages, towns and cities, constituted on both geographical and issue-based criteria (Toret 2015). The circles' purpose was to encourage debate and to politicise the public space, and at the same time to provide a communication strategy to spread messages that the party's founding members broadcast through their presence in the mainstream media. *Podemos* has also introduced digital technology for internal organisation purposes, such as selection processes for internal party posts or candidates, or defining key aspects of the political agenda. In the words of a member of *Podemos Valencia*, 'We use an assembly format to take decisions in our circles, and we use digital tools to take certain key decisions' (*Podemos* member 3).

The Catalan *Candidatura d'Unitat Popular* (CUP, or Popular Unity Candidacy) styles itself as an assembly-based party initiative. After 15M, the CUP adopted many of the procedures associated with the Mexican Zapatista movement (Muñoz Ramírez 2008), emphasising the importance of proposals coming from ordinary people: 'Nosaltres no us representem, vosaltres ens representeu a nosaltres' ('We don't represent ourselves; it is you who represent us'). David Fernández, member of the CUP, states:

> The traditional left said they act as intermediaries, mediating conflicts through parliament. We are not intermediaries for anybody. The PAH knows more about the problem of evictions, and the

feminist movement knows more about gender violence. Our job is to be at their service, not in front and not behind, and give them the space to speak for themselves in parliamentary committees, for example.[8]

The CUP encourages participation from both party members and non-members, holding public assemblies and committing to an open decision-making style. It defines itself as 'an assembly-based political party where there are no representatives, but rather delegates, and where decisions are discussed in depth in the places where the party exists' (CUP member 1).

Other political initiatives take a similar approach. For instance, the first stages of the *Barcelona en Común* political project, in June 2014, entailed listening to the demands of people in different neighbourhoods of the city. It organised open assemblies 'to find out what Barcelona's citizens really think and what their real political concerns are' (*Barcelona en Común* member 1). This platform aims 'to start a democratic process from the bottom up through citizen participation' (*Barcelona en Común* member 2) and 'to consolidate an open and plural process that gives the city back to its citizens and puts an end to the corporate colonisation of local politics' (*Barcelona en Común* member 2).

3) As a means for moving towards more direct, participatory forms of democracy, unconnected to the traditional parties

While some political parties seek to draw attention to the deficiencies in the political system, others aim to go one step further, turning the Spanish democratic system into a more participative model – perhaps even becoming a variant of direct democracy based on the use of digital technologies. Initiatives such as *Partido X* and *Partido Pirata* fall into this group; the Spanish branch of this now established pirate movement has already enjoyed electoral success in Germany and Scandinavia, although its presence and success in the polls are not so obvious in Spain.

The aim of this type of 'technopolitical' party is to dissolve representative party-based democracy and replace it with a more participatory democratic system. It would involve a type of decision making in which, through digital technologies, people can give their opinions about policies being developed or delegate their input to experts on the subject (which could in turn be revoked at any time). In its *Democracia y Punto* programme, *Partido X* presents a systemised democratic model that explores the extent of the political potential in digital communication tools. This programme highlights two key political processes needed to improve the democratic system: monitoring centres of power, and citizen participation in binding decision making.[9] Several points of the programme clearly identify participation through monitoring, controlling and vigilance, with society taking a supervisory role. An example is as follows: '[R]eal power must lie with the citizens and must be based on the distribution of control over government through numerous channels of collaboration, monitoring, participation and decision'.[10] It also urges, '[E]veryone must have access to the sources they need to be informed and control what others are doing in areas that might be relevant to their lives'.[11]

The *Partido X* political programme also advocates active participation in decision making through three mechanisms: wiki-participation (in matters of governance and legislation), permanent voting rights and binding referenda. These three pillars support a model of participatory-deliberative democracy for drawing up and debating legislative proposals and for introducing direct voting. *Partido X* specifically proposes mechanisms with which to alter the traditional processes of political intermediation, previously dominated by the traditional political parties (Subirats 2011, 2012). Their political initiative is a sophisticated experimental model in the relationships among politicians and citizens.[12]

For its part, LaboDemo (*Laboratorio Democrático*, the democratic laboratory) has developed innovative proposals for digital participation in *Podemos*. This initiative defines itself as 'a tool of change for the new democracy', working for 'a new emerging hyperconnected society creating new forms of collective intelligence networks'.[13] LaboDemo develops and promotes more direct methods of citizen participation for a range of organisations. Its achievements include setting up *Plaza Podemos* (Podemos Square) and the *Portal de Iniciativas Ciudadanas* (Citizens' Initiatives Portal), spaces for deliberation and voting on proposals within *Podemos*. LaboDemo also works with *Ahora Madrid* (the capital's ruling platform of various political groups) whose electoral manifesto included a full programme of participation promoted through the internet and digital technologies.[14]

The new parties and digital media

The political and economic crises have been major factors behind the explosion of new political parties. Many of the founders of these new groups have been involved in anti-austerity campaigns and are committed to horizontal practices associated with the early stages of 15M, particularly the *acampadas* and assemblies. It is equally evident, however, that digital technologies have allowed many activists to cross the once gaping divide between horizontalism and party-based, or vertical, forms of organisation. The question arises whether this axis is capable of capturing all the currents and tendencies at play in the political activism context. It seems clear that digital technologies are modifying the nature and potential for participation that political parties can offer, ameliorating the risks that horizontalist advocates associate with hierarchical party structures. Digital technologies, therefore, seem to be an area ripe for political experimentation. What, then, are the characteristics of this ecosystem and its constant stream of new political parties?

Pop-up political parties

Many of the new political parties in Spain are quick-fix, temporary or *pop-up* initiatives designed quite explicitly to take advantage of a moment of political crisis to advance a particular set of issues, such as disillusionment with the political class or internet censorship. This is not to say that the activists behind such initiatives do not want to create longer term and more lasting organisations. Rather, being able to organise very quickly via the internet means an immediate presence can be created, making the detailed fleshing out of a programme, or a manifesto, a matter for a later date.[15] It is in the nature of such evanescent political organisations that they can disappear just as quickly as they emerge; hence the pop-up analogy. In moments of deep political crisis, such as post-2011 Spain, political experimentation becomes the new norm. Some initiatives will succeed, while others will fail. The extraordinary success of *Podemos* has meant that some other parties with similar outlooks (*Partido X* in particular) have seen their fortunes wane as activists realise it is in their interests to consolidate their efforts at the polls.

Cheshire cat initiatives

The main purpose of many of these new parties is to achieve a specific goal, which if accomplished would immediately make the party redundant or obsolete. Even parties with more extensive programmes regard their initiatives to be of limited duration. *Partido X* defines itself as 'a citizen pressure group that aims to force a change in the democratic system' (*Partido X* member 3). To achieve this, the party seeks a 'citizens' covenant to demand a political system based on the principles of transparency, the real and permanent right to vote and wiki-legislation' (*Partido X* member 4). Once these changes have been implemented, whether by *Partido X* or another political party, this initiative will disappear.[16] *Partido Pirata* aims to establish a 'liquid democracy'[17] which would make political parties, including itself, obsolete. *Escaños en Blanco* says that its 'disappearance will come with electoral law reform that takes protest votes into account',[18] meaning that the system would formally recognise the blank or protest vote as a voter option without the need for a party to represent that choice. The idea of these parties' interventions in the political field is to bring about longer term structural, cultural or systemic changes that would effectively mean their work has been done. It is not yet clear whether *Podemos* or any of the municipal council coalition platforms will follow the same path. Given their electoral success, and what appears to be their more developed organisational capacity, their evolution might follow the pattern of classic left-wing parties. Some of the evanescent properties we are documenting here would begin to take shape along the lines seen in the history of other left-wing parties.

Anti-party parties

The new parties are 'anti-political' in that they both reject the hierarchical structure and discourse of traditional political parties and the neat division of labour among leaders, cadres and mass members. If there is one characteristic common to many of the current initiatives, it is their rejection of the figure of the 'politician' and the idea of the party as a vehicle for individuals to assume leadership positions. This has led to some interesting dilemmas, especially in light of party politics' traditional pursuit of charismatic leaders, not least for media purposes. *Podemos* must now find the right balance between the charismatic character of their media-friendly leader, Pablo Iglesias, and the circles and assemblies of the grassroots model. Most of our interviewees regarded such as figure as necessary for election purposes while acknowledging that it may pose problems now and in the future. They remained optimistic, however, that the grassroots participants would hold control over the movement's leading figures. As one activist noted, '*Podemos* is much more than Pablo Iglesias. The circles guarantee that this will continue to be the case' (*Podemos* member 1). Others argued that 'having such a media figurehead is a necessary evil' (*Podemos* member 2), and that 'Pablo Iglesias is crucial in this current stage, but once the grassroots activists are empowered he will no longer lead the movement' (*Podemos* member 3).

Partido X has grappled with alternatives to personality-centred politics, baulking at the idea of running named candidates in favour of anonymous candidates in an attempt to prioritise proposals over people. *Escaños en Blanco* runs named candidates, but only on the basis that they will renounce their seats if elected. Other parties, such as the CUP, elect their delegates in open assemblies, which also determine candidates' salaries and their length of term in office (with the option to stand for re-election only once).[19] In the discourse of all the parties there was a marked aversion to identifying one particular individual as a potential or actual leader. These are self-styled 'parties without politicians', or anti-party parties, in line with the Latin American model. This philosophy is clearly reflected in the definition *Barcelona en Común* (and numerous other local government groupings) gives itself as a 'citizens' platform',[20] a concept used to distance itself from any party political connotations.

Limited scope demands

One defining characteristic of the new parties is their clear vision of the issues that they want resolved. Unlike the more traditional parties, very few of them have what might be described as a full worldview or ideology. They believe that offering an integral alternative is less important than identifying a specific political objective to aim for. Their goals are to highlight citizens' disillusionment and to seek to 'pressurise politicians into carrying out their political tasks in a more ethical and respectful way'[21] (*Escaños en Blanco*); to promote 'universal and free access to Internet'[22] (*Partido Pirata*)[23]; or to 'take the citizens' decisions and votes directly to parliament'[24] (*Partido X*). Then again, *Podemos* might evolve in a different direction and present a traditional programme listing its demands, decided at the grassroots level or at least appearing to contain substantial grassroots contributions. *Barcelona en Común* and the other municipal platforms are also an exception on this point, since their perspectives at the polls, and subsequent success, have led them to draw up, using the participatory process, more detailed comprehensive programmes.

A means to an end

The new political parties are conceived as political tools, as opposed to vehicles for a distinctive ideology or conception of how we should live. Ideology is not generally a relevant feature of the new parties. Despite defining themselves as a 'left-wing' party, *Podemos* members did not relate to this identity. One argued, 'We do not believe in the traditional distinction of right and left [...]. We are simply those at the bottom of the system struggling against the elite' (*Podemos* member 4). For researcher Cristina Flesher Fominaya, '[I]t is precisely an *anti*-ideological stance, a refusal to self-define in terms of political ideologies ... that has marked an important element of the effective *Podemos* strategy' (Flesher Fominaya 2014b, p. 2). Interestingly, voter intention polls conducted in October and November 2014 pointed to *Podemos's* success when it separated its critique of the political and economic elites from the traditional leftist discourse. The ideological composition of voter intentions revealed how its anti-elitist position, highlighting the need to address the moral shortcomings of Spain's elites, is gaining electoral ground.[25] *Partido X*, in turn, states that its principles 'do not exactly match any ideology, doctrine or philosophy, but rather they are a pragmatic methodology',[26] whereas *Escaños en Blanco* defines itself as a 'non-ideological initiative'.[27]

The pragmatic and instrumental approach of today's party activists is in marked contrast to the type of activism associated with traditional mass political parties (Dalton 2002; Webb, Farrell & Holliday 2002). This in turn problematises the distinction between mainstream electoral politics and other types of participation that could be understood as complementary to the main business of politics. According to these interpretations, the traditional parties lie at the centre of the political process, which is clearly separate and differentiated from other types of civil society-based political participation. It is precisely the decline of political parties that makes political scientists so nervous about the prospects for democratic governance and representation (Whiteley 2011). In Spain what we find is a pragmatic instrumentalisation of the party formula itself. For activists, the party is 'one kind of political weapon', yet far from the only one (*Partido X* members 6 and 7). Indeed, as the activists' comments indicate, suspicion of the party format still remains, and attachment to the party is contingent upon, and mediated by, other strategic and tactical factors. ICTs have brought down the costs of setting up a party, but they also appear to have reduced the level of emotional attachment to them.

The impact of the new parties on party-based democracy

On the basis of what has been discussed so far, it is clear that those who fear the decline and potential disappearance of political parties within representative democratic systems can be confident that the party is not over yet. Indeed, given the proliferation of parties in crisis-afflicted societies such as Spain, this fear may be turned around to argue that the party has only just begun. What is also clear is that the traditional coordinates of the political party are changing rapidly. This in turn will have significant consequences for 'party-based democracy'. The question is: what will these consequences be?

First, it should be noted that in the Spanish case one of the main goals of the new parties is to draw attention to the deficiencies of democracy itself. One of the key slogans of 15M was *'Democracia real ¡ya!'* ('Real Democracy Now!'). What that slogan flagged was the belief that the existing democratic process was flawed in some of its basic aspects. 15M gave new value to democracy in a way that showed Europeans have not given up on democracy, even though they might express their disillusionment with the existing representative process (Wessels 2011). It seems that the point is to enrich and deepen the democratic practice so that, instead of equating it with the cyclical elections of politicians, it engages citizens on a daily basis. The result is a plethora of new political parties seeking to extend the democratic practice through Web 2.0 and peer-to-peer (P2P) technologies. The aim of many of these new parties is to reform the democratic institutions to ensure they work better. Certain analogies can be seen across Europe and in other parts of the world, such as the *Movimento 5 Stelle* (M5S, or Five Star Movement) in Italy and the recently formed WikiLeaks party in Australia. These are protest parties, but this does not mean that they are anti-democracy, the line often taken by some journalists and political analysts who tend to equate mass mobilisations with 'populist temptation' or anti-system tendencies (von Beyme 2011; Moffitt & Tormey 2014). These new parties seek to highlight the deficiencies affecting democracy and to encourage debate on how best to address them. Indeed, they might be understood as part of a broader effort of citizen initiatives to improve deliberation, provide greater opportunities for participation, and close the distance between politicians and citizens, and between state and civil society. Put another way, they pursue a more 'connective' way and style of doing politics (Bennett & Segerberg 2012). This might take the form of campaigns to encourage deliberative assemblies, participatory budgeting and so forth. In Spain it stems from the direct challenge to the hegemony of the main political parties, the political and economic elites, and the very system of representation.

Second, the new parties signal a general shift away from long-standing forms of political organisation to fleeting, evanescent and immediate styles of political interaction. The difference between direct or DIY participation and the type of politics associated with the traditional political parties is becoming increasingly difficult to discern (Diani & McAdam 2003; Day 2004; Mertes & Bello 2004; Castells 2012; Della Porta 2013). This reflects the changing ecology of political parties we referred to earlier. Until recently, setting up a political party was a time-consuming process. It demanded a great deal of energy and enthusiasm to launch an organisation that would require considerable funding and long hours of toil to be viable. This contrasted with other types of individualised collective action: protests, boycotts and demonstrations that were often one-off and event-based initiatives (Micheletti 2003). With the new digital technologies, the processes of organisation have become 'ridiculously easy' (Shirky 2009). The formula of how to create and structure a political party is undergoing a process of radical change. This does not mean that all political parties will have to change to survive, although much of the empirical evidence suggests that the parties themselves feel they must harness the new technologies as a matter of urgency if they do not want to fade away. What it does mean, however, is that the political landscape will be increasingly more complicated for voters to navigate as they are presented with an increasingly complex menu of options from which to choose – from the traditional political parties, to all manner of recently launched protest and specific interest parties. The new parties are part of a broader, more evanescent, liquid trend. Political parties will come and go from one election to the next, making our connection to them and what they represent weaker and less secure than the types of affiliation and affinity associated with the traditional parties, which often developed deep roots with their supporters.

Third, in light of the above point, the new political parties might be better conceptualised as part of a 'counter democracy' (Rosanvallon 2008) or a 'monitory democracy' (Keane 2009, 2013) rather than as a part of the traditional apparatus of state. As discussed earlier, the initial motivation and rationale for many new political parties was to disrupt the democratic process and draw attention to its limitations and shortcomings. Members of these parties are reluctant to see themselves as potential members of government or even of a coalition or alliance. On the other hand, events in Spain and the high levels of citizen disillusionment with the traditional party structures make the consolidation of significant electoral advances more likely in the short term. The Italian M5S is illustrative in this respect. The movement-party's self-image is that of an 'outsider', or to paraphrase Abensour (2011), of 'democracy against the state'. When faced with its own success in the general elections in 2013, M5S seemed to practically grind to a halt and appeared incapable of addressing the transition from a protest movement to a party in government. Nevertheless, we may eventually witness how the new parties play a key role in forcing significant changes in the nature and form of democratic government. In the case of Iceland, citizen mobilisation led to a constituent process that redefined the political process, reconstituted the central bank and brought corrupt politicians to justice (Castells 2012). 'Counter democracy' need not be theorised merely in terms of a force to put pressure on institutions of governance; it may become a force that transforms governance itself.

Obviously it is still early days to judge the impact the rise of *Podemos* and the municipal council platforms might have on the Spanish electoral landscape. *Podemos*'s success in the 2014 European elections came as a shock to the traditional parties. Many of the demands of 15M and the new parties, such as more and better citizen participation, changes to mortgage legislation and removal of privileges for parties and politicians, are yet to have an impact on the programmes of the two main political parties (PP and PSOE). Where they have had a more tangible effect is in the political party membership model. The new parties are large plural organisations with open, or practically open, membership policies. Many of them charge no fee, and the registration process for participating in debates, primaries and candidate selection is usually a formality, if indeed it exists at all. In turn, this is affecting the perception of how a political party could, and should, organise itself internally and is influencing traditional parties that now feel obliged to open up and democratise their structures.

Although the influence of 15M and the new parties on the traditional parties' programmes is slow, they do seem to be having an immediate effect on the way the parties are organised; the old parties have to make efforts to connect, to foster members' engagement and to introduce a battery of alternatives in order to retain their support and attract new followers. The once exclusive 'private party' model is coming increasingly under strain as the 'street parties', through their inclusive model of recruiting and organising, attract new members.

Conclusions

The analysis of the Spanish case suggests that political parties are not endangered, at least for the present. Even in crisis-afflicted contexts, there is a palpable appetite to create and build new political parties. We are unlikely to witness a shift from traditional democracy to 'post-representative' democracy with the decline of the political party. The shift from a typically slow, measured and predictable style of politics, associated with representative democracy, to a fleeting, evanescent politics that resonates rather than represents, does seem to have had a considerable impact on the nature and kind of political parties emerging in this evolving political landscape. We do not believe that this metamorphosis is simply a response to the contingent crisis that has left its mark on countries like Spain with the fallout from the global financial crisis. It is as much a story about digital media and the new opportunities it affords activists as it is about declining trust in the representative structures, which is so much in evidence in countries affected by crisis and corruption. What political analysts must not ignore is the revolutionary potential of the new digital media to create groups and organisations with an ease that was inconceivable until very recently. Just as our own personal relations are being transformed by social media groups and their boundless opportunities for communication, so our relationship with politics is changing. For our purposes, this means we need to rethink political parties as not just the means for ensuring the rotation of elites, as described by minimalist models of democracy, but as part of a broader political ecology that is challenging these classical models of democracy and the traditional party.

Some questions obviously remain unanswered. Given that some of the new protest parties are beginning to resonate with sectors of the electorate, does this mean we can expect a change in the style and substance of democratic politics? Is it conceivable that democracy itself will be redrawn in some new important way, reducing or even removing altogether the separation between elites and citizens, as *Podemos* promises? Or will the new parties tread the 'populist left' path, promising more citizen participation, 'ethical governance' and 'bottom-up initiatives', while at the same time delivering an all-too-familiar party-based or even presidential rule? Whatever the case, it seems clear that with the social movements' arrival on the party scene and the consolidation of this space as a new fruitful testing ground, the coordinates of Spanish democracy are set to change in ways that are significant not only for Spain, but for representative democratic systems more generally.

Notes

1 The party register (in Spanish) can be consulted at: https://servicio.mir.es/nfrontal/webpartido_politico.html.
2 A total of 37 city or town council initiatives affiliated in April 2015, including *Ahora Madrid, Marea Atlántica, Málaga Ahora, Participa Sevilla, Zaragoza en Común, Valencia en Común* and *Castellón en Movimiento.*

3 In *El País*, "*Podemos: Un partido sin carnés y en construcción*" (26 May 2014) http://politica.elpais.com/politica/2014/05/26/actualidad/1401133012_502908.html.

4 Arturo Puente, Joäo França and Enric Català interviewed Ada Colau in *ElDiario.es*: "Ada Colau: '*No queremos ir al ayuntamiento para tener algún concejal, queremos ganar*'" (28 June 2014) www.eldiario.es/catalunya/Ada -Colau-Guanyem-Barcelona-queremos-Pepito-Grillo_0_275772433.html.

5 http://esconsenblanc.org.

6 http://escanos.org/sobre-escanos-en-blanco/.

7 http://partidox.org/programa/.

8 Interview (in Spanish) in *Atlántica* (20 August 2013) www.atlanticaxxii. com/1753/david-fernandez-cabeza-de-lista-de-la-cup-de-la-crisis-salimos-ma s-libres-o-mas-esclavos.

9 The *Democracia y Punto* programme refers 19 times to the concepts of control, vigilance and monitoring, while the concept of participation is mentioned on 29 occasions.

10 http://partidox.org/sobre-ley-de-transparencia/.

11 http://partidox.org/sobre-ley-de-transparencia/.

12 This initiative is founded on the belief that internet and ICTs allow people to imagine new forms of citizen participation, a stance that is reflected in three proposals: 1) Wiki-legislation and wiki-governance; 2) the right to a real and permanent vote; and 3) obligatory and binding referenda. Wiki-legislation and wiki-governance are directly linked to the participatory and transparent preparation of legislative material. The initiative proposes to turn the legislative process into a space for open collaboration of citizens following models such as the *Gabinete Digital* (Digital Cabinet) in the Brazilian state of Rio Grande do Sul and the Better Reykavik project in Iceland. The right to a real and permanent vote would open up possibilities for citizens to coparticipate in parliamentary decisions, linking the parliamentary vote to the possibility of citizens' obtaining part of the representative quota in parliament. With a ratio of 35 million voters for 350 members, the participation of 100,000 citizens in a given vote would imply transferring one parliamentary seat to the vote from outside parliament (Jurado Gilabert 2013). This mechanism is intended to become 'a means of effective citizen surveillance that obliges politicians to do their job properly, back up their decisions with data and rigourous studies and provide citizens with opportune explanations on every legislative proposal'. Finally, the obligatory and binding referendum as a mechanism for direct participation would be used in 'exceptional cases such as structural laws (constitution, organic laws, etc.) or in cases in which the government ignores questions that citizens consider essential (through popular legislative initiatives)'.

13 http://labodemo.net/acerca-de-labodemo/.

14 See the programme at: https://conoce.ahoramadrid.org/wp-content/uploads/2015/04/AHORAMADRID_Programa_Municipales_2015.pdf (In Spanish. The section about participation is on p. 24).

15 The exponential growth of the new parties through Facebook is evident in the case of *Partido X* and *Podemos*. One study concluded that in its first few months of activity in 2013, the *Partido X* Facebook page (www.facebook. com/PartidoXPartidodelFuturo) became the second most popular in Spain in terms of new content creation. The study (in Spanish) by the Interactive

Advertising Bureau (IAB) is available at: www.iabspain.net/wp-content/up loads/downloads/2013/11/Informe_comparativo_Partidos_Politicos_Espa%C3%B1oles_Facebook.pdf.

In 2014, the launch of *Podemos* was even more spectacular, reaching a total of 911,712 followers by December of that year. This figure is particularly striking when compared with Facebook followers for the PP (79,513) and the PSOE (75,435).

16 http://partidox.org/preguntas-frecuentes/.
17 The Liquid Democracy organisation; available at: https://liqd.net/en.
18 www.facebook.com/esconsenblanc.
19 http://cup.cat/noticies/participacio.
20 https://barcelonaencomu.cat/ca/principis.
21 www.facebook.com/esconsenblanc/info.
22 https://partidopirata.es/conocenos/programa.
23 www.pp-international.net/about.
24 http://partidodeinternet.es/.
25 In October 2014, polls conducted by the Centre of Social Research (CIS) placed *Podemos* as the third most popular party Spain, with 22.5 per cent of voters expressing a preference for it. A *Metroscopia* poll, carried out in November and December 2014, calculated *Podemos*'s popularity at 25 per cent, above that of the PP (20 per cent) and very close to the popularity of the PSOE (27.7 per cent). The CIS revealed the diverse composition of *Podemos*'s voters, who come not only from those who usually abstain (15.5 per cent), spoil their ballot papers (36.4 per cent), or who are from the left (45.6 per cent from *Izquierda Unida* – United Left– and between 27.4 per cent and 28.8 per cent from the PSOE), but who are also from more conservative ideological positions (between 27.4 per cent and 28.8 per cent from the liberal UPyD party, between 6.6 and 9.8 per cent from the Catalan regionalist conservative party CiU, and what is most surprising, 6 per cent of PP voters). This poll showed that 6 per cent of those who voted for the PP in the previous general elections in 2011 intended to vote for *Podemos* in 2015. This percentage is higher in the *Metroscopia* poll, which estimated that 8 per cent of previous PP voters were considering voting for *Podemos*. Celeste-Tel polls put this percentage at 24.7 per cent. Information available at: CIS October poll: http://ep00.epimg.net/descargables/2014/11/05/f65f19988a09564864ddb9414be2f785.pdf (Accessed 12 December 2014.) November and December *Metroscopia* polls: http://elpais.com/tag/metros copia/a/ , www.metroscopia.org/ and http://blogs.elpais.com/metroscopia/2014/12/barometro-electoral-diciembre-2014.html November 2014 Celeste-Tel poll: www.eldiario.es/politica/ENCUESTA-cuarta-Podemos-proce de-PP_0_326868090.html (accessed 13 December 2014).
26 http://partidox.org/preguntas-frecuentes/.
27 http://escanos.org/.

3 The appearance of monitoring as an emerging political dynamic

The use of new digital communication tools by activist and civil society groups has led to the emergence and consolidation of new forms of citizen participation. The publication of secret information from major political powers by such organisations as WikiLeaks, and the capacity to mobilise new social movements organised by such networks as Occupy Wall Street, #YoSoy132 and 15M, are becoming increasingly visible. Such actions are bolstered by the impact of online petitions and votes via digital platforms such as ThePetitionSite, Change.org and Avaaz as well as new voices in alternative media such as Indymedia. All these examples share an emerging political dynamic: they are helping to consolidate the public monitoring of political and economic power centres.

In the Spanish context, growing citizen political mobilisation presents a series of objectives that are framed within the general monitoring process. Among the main aims set out by the various platforms and initiatives, to be examined throughout this chapter, are the following: 1) modifying the media and political agenda; 2) adding to the plurality of points of view; 3) promoting transparency; and, finally, 4) denouncing those responsible for the political and economic crises. These goals are shared by numerous active civil society groups. In promoting them, a series of initiatives have been designed to scrutinise the centres of power. These questions come to mind. How can the processes of citizen scrutiny be theoretically framed in contemporary political theory? What is the potential and novelty of the political monitoring process? What actors and processes make up this dynamic? To answer these questions, we explore the theoretical framework of monitory democracy.

Monitory democracy: political transformation in communication-saturated societies

Monitory democracy interprets the present political situation as a time of change in which monitoring takes root as an emerging form of political participation (Schudson 1998). Monitoring, defined as the exercise of public scrutiny of power centres and relations, is considered to be on the rise as a result of the potential provided by the new digital communication structure (Gripsrud 2009; Sousa, Agante & Gouveia 2010), which is understood to favour the consolidation of counter-powers against the institutionalised power of governments and business corporations (Keane 2009, 2013; Rosanvallon 2008).

Monitory democracy implies that representative democracies, as diverse as the United States, India, New Zealand and the members of the European Union, are facing the emergence of new political dynamics that alter the 'architecture of self-government' with regard to political parties, elections and parliament. Although still essential, these are losing ground to peripheral actors that subject the centres of accumulated power to constant scrutiny and evaluation (Keane 2009, pp. 686–692). This scrutiny takes place in public, addresses issues of public interest and is able to influence political centres in numerous ways, including changing government decisions, expanding the media and political agendas and bringing about resignations and rectifications.

The phenomena of citizen disillusionment with representative structures, parties, parliament and elections (Crouch 2004; Rosanvallon 2008) are not understood as crises of politics, but rather as processes of change (Keane 2013; Rosanvallon 2008). Within this change, monitoring has emerged as an outstanding form of political participation. Apart from voting in elections, counterpowers have the opportunity to closely examine the decisions their representatives make and to raise the alarm when something appears to be wrong. This consolidation of the monitoring processes cannot be understood without studying the new patterns in digital communication that allow the existence of 'something like a 'parallel' government of publics' (Keane 2005, p. 19). Moreover, this communications architecture is considered to foster the porosity of power centres. Counterpowers and power-scrutinising mechanisms build up an ever-growing arsenal of instruments to assess and value power holders' actions through very heterogeneous monitoring processes.

The new communication landscape is triggering fundamental changes in many spheres, particularly in the field of political communication. Since the appearance of the internet, the media world seems to be constantly creating networks or mechanisms that change the way citizens communicate and impact on the communication landscape revolving around the democratic system. Social networks are all taking up more space in our everyday lives: Facebook; microblogging sites like Twitter; voice, text and image communication tools such as Skype and the thousands of different blogs on platforms like Blogger and WordPress. Periods of scarce information, one-directional communication processes, sluggish information transmission and control of what information should be made public all seem to have been left behind as these new forms of communication expand and the complex media scene is consolidated (McNair 2006). The traditional media – press, radio and television – are also present in this media landscape, resulting in an unprecedented miscellany of communication tools (Sifry 2011).

We live in revolutionary times of abundant communication in which numerous media innovations and digital communication tools are arousing much interest. In the political field, the flourishing of numerous exciting political dynamics is altering the landscape of our democracies, often for the better. This abundance of communication nourishes monitory democracy, whose most striking trends include scrutiny of the centres of power. Aside from the limitations and problems associated with the new digital landscape (Keane 2013; Hindman 2009; Chester 2007), it is becoming more difficult to set the information agenda, control information or hide news in a time marked by a plurality of actors able to express their views through many different channels (Casero-Ripollés 2010).

It is no surprise that the verb 'monitor' is now widely used to describe the process of systematic examination and control of the content or quality of a procedure or a decision (Keane 2009). The value and meaning of the concept of monitoring applied to monitory democracy is two-fold: on the one hand, it covers the idea of *public scrutiny* processes, and on the other it embraces the term 'monitor' as a piece of *audiovisual apparatus*. It involves observance as in watching (monitoring) and at the same time observance through numerous audiovisual devices (monitors or screens). Monitoring is, therefore, considered to have the capacity to extend political processes beyond the cycle of voting at election time and is a growing presence in democratic systems like that of Spain.

Underlying the monitoring phenomenon is the idea that, in an increasingly complex society, there will be more political demands and also more representatives who take up these demands and defend them. These include not only representatives elected in the polls, but also civil society actors who put themselves forward to represent specific interests and who share a political landscape with an increasing number of concerns and voices (García-Marzá 2008, 2013). The immediate effect of this process is that citizens frequently incorporate the basic questions of 'who gets what, when and how in this world?' into the public sphere (Keane 2013). Cases of corruption, malpractice and abuse of power are publicly denounced in a growing demand by citizens for greater accountability in the centres of power (Gutiérrez-Rubí 2011; Feenstra & Casero-Ripollés 2014).

Three main fields of monitoring: governmental, civic and shared

The heterogeneity of the scrutiny processes taking shape in monitory democracy raises a basic question: how can these processes be identified and differentiated in national and international political spheres? The literature to date has mainly examined the growing relevance of monitoring processes and their relation with the new communication environment (Keane 2009, 2013). The concept offers a new perspective from which to observe recent changes in political communication and democracy, but we have yet to see an approach enabling such public scrutiny processes to be contextualised from the practical point of view.

Prior to this discussion, it should be noted that the categorisation presented here has its own issues associated with establishing typologies which are necessarily somewhat arbitrary due to the selection of political elements and processes that by definition are dynamic (Weber 1978). The typologies established here highlight the most relevant and differentiating characteristics of various monitoring processes. As such, they cannot fully embrace all their richness and heterogeneity, and some types or examples defined here might overlap. For this reason, it must be remembered that monitoring is characterised precisely by its dynamic nature in which multiple actors and monitoring forms can be intertwined. This does not invalidate, however, the urgent need for a categorisation of monitory democracies with which to differentiate and understand the multiple political tendencies taking shape in varied political contexts.

The notion of monitory democracy raises an initial question: who exactly are the monitoring *agents* (Munck 2006)? This question is linked to a second one that is the focus of our attention in this chapter: what types of monitoring can be identified?

We can identify three main sectors around which monitoring is organised – according to the leading actor or organisation behind it: governmental, shared and civic monitoring. The first of these is linked to government institutions, the second involves collaboration between government institutions and civil society actors and the third is the purview of citizens and society. The main aspect common to all three types is that they all promote public scrutiny in multiple political and economic spheres and centres of power. Obviously, the main difference lies in where the monitoring is actually done, although we will also show significant variations in the type and form of monitoring each one promotes and on which spheres they focus their attention.

Governmental monitoring is defined by the processes that government institutions put in place to scrutinise the pillars of representative democracy: judicial independence, public access to information, respect for human rights, implementation of public policies and so on (Munck 2009). They are promoted by diverse organisations operating at different levels (regional, national or global) and are designed to evaluate, according to specific standards, the democratic situation in countries. The results are published in a series of reports (Bjornlund 2004). Organisations undertaking this type of monitoring include the Office for Democratic Institutions and Human Rights, part of the Organisation for Security and Cooperation in Europe (OSCE), the Electoral Assistance Division of the United Nations and the Human Development Report Team within the United Nations Development Programme (UNDP).

There are also many examples of public organisations in this field that use the internet to spread information about their actions, measures and public spending in order to increase transparency. These initiatives are related to 'open government' (Perritt 1997; Lathrop & Ruma 2010). Notable examples from the United States are Recovery.gov, an official government website where citizens can track government investments of public funds, and Data.gov, which provides information on government operations in environmental, education, economic and many other fields. Similar initiatives are found in other countries such as India, whose India.gov.in website is particularly noteworthy.

Shared monitoring is based on collaborations of varying intensities between government intuitions and civil society to promote public scrutiny processes. Such collaborations are indispensable in developing this type of scrutiny, the main focus of which is the representative system and its central pillars. One example is election monitoring, which began to spread at the end of World War II (1945) especially in recent or fragile democracies, and is now a common process in many countries.

The Carter Center in the United States performs this type of scrutiny through its outstanding electoral observation and control section. Activists, election law experts and political scientists collaborate with political representatives to ensure that the election processes in numerous countries operate openly and honestly. The Center's work has proved to be essential in creating some basic international election monitoring principles, which have been debated within international institutions such as the Electoral Assistance Division of the UN and national bodies like the US National Democratic Institute for International Affairs.

Initiatives of collaboration between government organisations and civil society actors, with the aim of promoting scrutiny and citizen participation, are visible in other ways, as they promote the incorporation of new voices or bottom-up participation dynamics. One outstanding example is the participatory budgets in Latin America, which have proved to be a good way of collaborating and encouraging dependency between politicians and citizens, promoting new forms of participation (Cabannes 2004). Although this type of intervention comes closer to promoting collective participation than pure monitoring, it is also a type of scrutiny because it oversees public investment.

The third type of monitoring differs in that it is undertaken by citizens and civil society using the opportunities provided by the new digital communications environment. This type of *civic monitoring* aims to publicly denounce abuses of power or highlight citizens' demands on issues such as lack of transparency and possible imbalances in the democratic system.

Although all three monitoring modes are essential to the monitory democracy model (Keane 2009), in this chapter we focus on the third mode for three reasons. First, this type of monitoring is directly associated with civil society participation. Second, it is innovative in the way it changes and reshapes the dynamics of citizen participation in the digital environment. Third, civic monitoring is the type of political scrutiny that has emerged most forcefully in our context. It has also emerged in very different channels, many of which have appeared precisely because of failings or shortcomings associated with the processes of governmental monitoring in Spain (e.g. problems associated with the Court of Audit or the Bank of Spain).

Civic monitoring is highly varied and takes many forms because it is the result of technological developments and creative innovations by activists (Earl & Kimport 2011). For this reason, it is useful to differentiate four basic types of civic monitoring in order to contextualise the many examples and cases of public scrutiny that arise in the digital context. These four classifications are explored in Table 3.1.

Typology of civic monitoring

Civic monitoring can take several forms, such as public denunciation, political demands from the periphery, expansion of voting or online petitions on issues of public interest via various digital platforms. Monitoring should increase the number of viewpoints on the fundamental topics of political discourse as well as the number of issues discussed, especially those left off the agendas of the political parties and the mass media (Casero-Ripollés & Feenstra 2012). Monitoring aims to end the

Table 3.1 Monitoring Processes

Basic monitoring areas	Definition	Types of monitoring
Governmental monitoring	Monitoring dependent on governmental institutions. Scrutiny is applied by public organisations to assess the situation of political structures as regards human rights. New communication tools are used to improve processes of government transparency.	1) Assessment and reports about democracy and human rights 2) Introduction of the principle of transparency (linked to the concept of open government)
Shared monitoring	Monitoring through colla-boration between govern-ment institutions and civil society to develop pro-cesses of public scrutiny.	1) Election monitoring 2) Participatory budgets
Civic monitoring	Monitoring led by citizens and civil society actors; public scrutiny of ques-tions of public interest and centres of political and economic power.	1) Watchdog function 2) Extracting and leak-ing secret or hidden information 3) Extending voices: alternative journalism 4) Extending representa-tion beyond parliaments

secrecy surrounding certain decisions or institutions by delving into the digital space to gather information previously kept offstage. In summary, civic monitoring takes the four following forms (see Table 3.2):

• Watchdog function
• Extracting and leaking secret or hidden information
• Extending voices: alternative journalism
• Extending representation beyond parliaments.

These monitoring processes are clearly entwined: one actor may raise several forms of scrutiny, just as a specific monitoring process may be led by various actors. This basic distinction can be used to identify several scrutiny processes that are now taking shape. There appear to be many initiatives to monitor the centres of power in the recent Spanish political context. The lack of transparency in numerous

Table 3.2 Types of Civic Monitoring

Types of civic monitoring	Definition	Key concept
Watchdog function	Supervising the behaviour of centres of power; denunciation of abuses, injustices and malpractice	Control
Extracting and leaking secret or hidden information	Extraction and diffusion of secret information to promote transparency	Leaks
Extending voices: alternative journalism	Emergence of alternative channels for new circulation beyond mainstream media, and so increasing the range of topics to be included on the public agenda and in political discourse	Information (news)
Extending representation beyond parliaments	Extension of political representation by civil society groups demanding democratic regeneration. They are led mainly by new social movements organised and mobilised through the internet. E-tactics, developed through digital technologies, and particularly online petitions, play a major role.	Mobilisation

public institutions, together with the search for those responsible for the political and economic crisis, have strengthened those parts of civil society that specialise in promoting the public scrutiny of power. In recent years, civil society and citizens in general have debated a diverse range of questions: the day-to-day activities of public representatives; corruption in the management of public budgets; malfunctioning representative structures; the close relationships between certain politicians and large corporations; murky practices in political party funding; the aggressive business policies of the banks; the disproportional electoral system; and many more. All these issues have come to light in the public sphere as a result of external pressure by citizens (Casero-Ripollés & Feenstra 2012).

The watchdog function

The watchdog function involves controlling the behaviour of centres of political and economic power and denouncing abuses, injustices and malpractice. Control is a key concept in this modality. The watchdog function has traditionally been an essential role of journalism (Casero-Ripollés 2008). The way a political system behaves is controlled through the news, by informing the public of abuses made by institutions of power. Journalists play a part in protecting the public interest and the common good. This scrutiny is a fundamental pillar of the democratic system: One clear historical example is the Watergate scandal.

The economic crisis facing mainstream media is jeopardising this practice by undermining journalistic independence and redirecting its activity to more commercially profitable fields, weakening the ability of conventional journalism to monitor the centres of power (Kovach & Rosenstiel 2007). Although the role of watchdog has traditionally been attributed to journalism, its scope is now spreading beyond journalistic boundaries. In the current environment, any individual or organisation has the potential to act as a watchdog, thanks to digital technologies that have ended journalism's monopoly of public scrutiny in the centres of power. Citizens and civil society groups can now act as guardians against inefficiency and injustice by using the internet and social media to denounce illegal or immoral practices in the political and economic systems.

A prime example of this type of monitoring in the Spanish context is linked to the new specialised platforms set up to scrutinise both specific institutions of power (e.g. the senate, parliament, politicians, banks and so on) and specific controversial decisions or actions. These are civil initiatives in which ordinary citizens become specialists in tracking politicians' actions, extracting information, drawing up reports, sharing information or transcribing information in open formats. Some of these initiatives are ongoing and stable – for example, *Qué hacen los diputados* (What Members of Parliament Do), *Civio, Sueldos Públicos* (Public Salaries), *OpenKratio* or *Cuentas Claras* (Clear Accounts) or they function as processes in which various groups work together on an ad hoc basis to examine a specific problem (see Table 3.3).

Collaborative monitoring platforms have mushroomed since 2011, when *Qué hacen los diputados* first appeared, following models such as opencongress.com and openpolis.it (Tascón & Quintana 2012). This platform aims to closely track the activities of members of parliament and then publish the information. It defines itself as 'a group of people interested in politics who think digital tools can help us to monitor the work politicians do'.[1] *Qué hacen los diputados* has an application where citizens can engage collaboratively in various tasks, such as following a politician and posting the information they gather; scrutinising the official state bulletins; correcting and polishing the information collected by other contributors; or editing information on collaborative

Table 3.3 Types of Monitoring Platforms

Platform	Mission	Website	Founded in
Adopta un senador (Adopt a senator)	Publishes politicians' asset statements in open format	http://derecho-internet. org/node/569	2011
Qué hacen los diputados	Scrutinises politicians' daily activities	http://quehacenlosdiputa dos.net/	2011
Cuentas Claras	Comprehensive exploration of opaque political party funding methods	http://cuentas-claras.org/	2011
Civio.org	Examines specific policies: pardons, accountability, tax investment and the relationship between institutions and citizens	www.civio.es/	2012
Sueldos Públicos	Scrutinises politicians' remuneration and abuses of office	www.sueldospublicos.com/	2012
Open Kratio	Promotes open government	http://openkratio.org/	2011

spaces like 15MPedia or Wikipedia. Since it first appeared, *Qué hacen los diputados* has published numerous reports containing detailed information about politicians' activities. A similar platform is *Civio*, an initiative inspired by MySociety,[2] which began in February 2012, in defence of 'information transparency, accountability and openness of data through the use of technology'.[3] This platform has collaborated with *Qué hacen los diputados* since December 2012 and specialises in publicly monitoring specific matters, such as the granting of pardons, transparency of local, regional and state administrations, and public assistance services. Another relevant project is *Sueldos Públicos*, which campaigns for transparency and clear information on politicians' incomes and public spending. Activists linked to 15M set up *Cuentas Claras* to scrutinise political party funding. Finally, the collective behind the

OpenKratio platform pursues open government and the opening up of public data through numerous initiatives and technical assessment projects. In addition to these platforms, which continuously monitor certain centres of power, collaborative monitoring processes have also emerged to examine or debate particular issues through citizen cooperation. A good illustration of this process is the 15MpaRato campaign,[4] which combined the possibilities offered by *crowdfunding* and *crowdsourcing* for collaborative work. The campaign helped bring to justice both former IMF President Rodrigo Rato and the board members involved in the Bankia IPO. This initiative began by gathering information on the case with the collaboration of internet users and eventually led to a legal court case. Bringing this case to court required some €15,000. An appeal was launched through a crowdfunding campaign and, in less than 24 hours, raised €18,359 from 965 donations. Within days the complaint was filed (Tascón & Quintana 2012).[5]

Extracting secret information and whistle-blowers

Another monitoring process, particularly relevant in the Web 2.0 context, is that performed by organisations and digital platforms to investigate or gather secret or hidden information. The activists carrying out this type of monitoring, often with links to hacktivism (Lievrouw 2011), thrive in the space the internet provides for them to develop and grow. They also create safe spaces where whistle-blowers can leak information about malpractices, the abuse of power and corruption without trace. Publishing leaked information to promote transparency is at the core of this type of monitoring.

WikiLeaks may be regarded as one of the prime examples of this type of monitoring leaking information using digital technologies. The organisation first emerged in 2006 but gained international notoriety in 2010 with the broadcast of the video *Collateral Murder* (Feenstra 2012). The video showed an aerial attack on Baghdad on 12 July 2007 in which two US helicopters, AH-64 Apaches, opened fire on a group of civilians, killing twelve people. The stated goal of the WikiLeaks platform is to reduce corruption and consolidate a stronger democracy through public scrutiny (Sifry 2011).[6] Its search for secret information drives and enriches its activity (Díaz & Lozano 2013). WikiLeaks has initiated some of the most notable and well-known monitoring processes in the past few years by releasing secret information about the wars in Afghanistan and Iraq as well as documents from the US State Department. The mainstream media have played an essential role in this process by evaluating, contextualising and eventually widely publishing information passed on to them from WikiLeaks. The *New York Times, The Guardian, Le Monde* and *El País* have provided a voice for civic monitoring by extending the scope and social impact of this leaked information.

Similar platforms have also sprung up in Spain, creating safe channels and 'mailboxes' where people can report fraud, abuses of power or cases of corruption. One example is the citizen platform *Fíltrala* (Leak it), which is part of the international *Associated Whistleblowing Press* network. This platform, working with media such as *Diagonal, La Marea, Eldiario.es* and *Mongolia*, defends the importance of 'the public helping to restore the active role of the media as overseers of the powers that be'.[7] Another similar platform is BuzónX (MailboxX), directly linked to *Partido X*, which has uncovered such significant cases of power abuse as the 'black' credit cards and the Blesa emails in the Caja Madrid corruption scandal.[8] The leaking of Blesa's emails exposed abuse by around 80 bankers, politicians and trade union leaders who, in their capacity as the bank's directors or executives, had been issued 'black' credit cards for personal expenses (e.g. holidays, hotels, restaurants and other expenses). Between 2003 and 2012, a combined total of €15 million was supplied.

These platforms and mailboxes give citizens the opportunity to leak secret information through secure virtual spaces protected by state-of-the-art cryptographic technologies. The proliferation of these systems may also attract more whistle-blowers to leak information about events in both political and economic centres of power, bringing hidden information out into the open (Calvo 2015). Insiders who release information about abuses being carried out in the institutions or organisations in which they work, or have worked, are particularly useful. Daniel Ellsberg's classic leak of what became known as the Pentagon Papers appears to have made a forceful comeback recently. Whistle-blower Bradley Manning, the main WikiLeaks source who was arrested after hacker Adrian Lamo reported him to the authorities, is an example. Another case is 'Spider Truman', the pseudonym of a former employee of the Italian Chamber of Deputies who published *The Secrets of the Caste of Montecitorio State* in 2012.[9] First on Facebook and later on a blog, his writing revealed compromising information about Italian MPs' expenses and misuse of public funds. In Spain, revelations by Herve Falciani had a significant impact. While working for the Swiss bank HSBC, this Italian-French systems engineer gathered information on more than 130,000 tax evaders, which he eventually leaked in what became known in the media as the 'Falciani list'. Falciani fell foul of the Swiss legal system for violating bank secrecy laws and fled to Spain where he was arrested. Eventually the National

Court released him but, because of his collaboration with the Spanish and French legal systems, the Court rejected Switzerland's extradition request. Following the publication of the Falciani list, tax evasion cases have been uncovered and denounced in several countries. This affair also highlighted the lack of transparency in the HSBC banking system in Switzerland and the methods used to hide the assets of business executives, politicians, sportsmen and women, arms and drug dealers and warlords. The bank's role in helping them evade taxes was exposed.[10] Information from the Falciani list has enabled states like Spain to recover millions of euros in unpaid taxes.[11]

The expansion of voices: consolidation of new forms of journalism

Digital technologies have opened up alternative channels to broadcast news beyond the mainstream media, strengthening monitoring through the spread of information. This process, together with public empowerment, has led to the multiplication of information producers in the digital landscape. Mass self-communication has made it easier for users not only to consume but also to produce and disseminate information autonomously (Castells 2009). The journalistic and political elites' monopoly of information management is coming to an end (Casero-Ripollés 2010; Davis 2010) and is giving way to a much more open and competitive scenario on the internet.

The proliferation of activists using new information online has provided a platform for topics previously kept off the public agenda: news previously passed over by the mainstream media can no longer be silenced (Tewksbury & Rittenberg 2012). Ultimately, the mainstream media may have no choice but to cover issues that civil society actors have put into circulation and made socially visible (Feenstra 2012; Bakardjieva 2012), expanding the range of issues that can capture the public's attention. Getting an issue onto the public agenda is vital to shaping public opinion – it is the first step towards citizens' political participation (McCombs 2004). Spreading news and extending the public agenda are, therefore, prime methods of civic monitoring designed to prevent the silencing of issues relevant to the public interest.

The new internet information actors have a clear presence in these recent alternative forms of journalism and may be classified either as radical media or citizen journalism. Radical media are online sites publishing alternative political and social news items that are generally excluded from or downplayed in the mainstream media (Downing 2001). These sites are the preferred channels for disseminating the opinions and concerns of activists and the more politically mobilised civil society groups.

Their agendas tend to be associated with the interests of social movements, and they reject the subordination of the institutional agenda imposed by political and economic systems and reproduced by the mainstream media (Della Porta 2011). Radical media action becomes a form of monitoring by helping to extend the range of issues being discussed and by diversifying the public agenda. Their activity aims to capture citizens' attention to promote successful activism, as this is the only way to raise the social profile of such issues (Lomicky & Hogg 2010).

One of the first and most widely known examples of alternative media is *Indymedia*, which emerged in 1999 following the anti-NATO protests in Seattle. Its original structure has expanded to include dozens of independent media centres, now forming an alternative media collective publishing in eight languages (Pickard 2006; Garcelon 2006; Flesher Fominaya 2014a). Such spaces provide alternative channels for creating and broadcasting news items that differ from or extend news in the mass media. They are essentially differentiated by their economic and political independence. Radical media are, therefore, constantly playing a monitoring role.

In recent years, alternative journalism projects have also taken root in Spain. They are defined in terms of their funding, internal organisation and transmission channel – that is, in the way they do journalism. One notable case is *Diagonal*, a critical and independent media that defines its collaborators as 'communication activists' and is organised along assembly principles. This newspaper aims to give a voice to social and alternative movements, and it also endeavours to secure financing to guarantee its independence. It is funded by subscriptions and limits its advertising revenue to 20 per cent of its total income, only accepting advertisements from companies that follow ethical criteria. Launched in 2005, this newspaper overhauled its structures and sections in 2009, and in 2011 it consolidated its presence on the internet.

Another series of internet media have also emerged in recent years and, although they are heterogeneous and not all may be described as fully alternative, they all defend a style of journalism based on the principle of independence from political and economic powers. These new initiatives have extended the range of voices heard in the journalistic landscape and have brought in new actors who have an effect on shaping public opinion. Recently established written digital journalism projects include *Periodismo Humano, La Marea, porCausa, Rebelión* and *Cuartopoder*. Table 3.4 shows that the *raison d'être* of these media platforms is to defend transparency and the citizens' rights to access diverse sources of information about what is happening in the centres of power; they are, therefore, also directly associated with monitoring activity.

Table 3.4 Media Platform Goals

Media	Goals *(taken from the media's own sites)*	Year founded and website
Diagonal	We are a critical and independent media. We are communication activists. We try to avoid being swept along by the fast pace of keeping permanently up to date; we are not interested in throw-away news. We prefer to stop and analyse what is happening, interpret it and offer frameworks of meaning that help us to find the right direction and change the rules of the game. We do not have most of the solutions, but we do have the questions.	2005; remodelled in 2011 to enter the digital environment. www.diagonalperiodico.net
Periodismo Humano	We want to bring back the social function of journalism and the concept of public service for citizens – not to serve particular economic or political interests. Information is not simply a tradeable asset or business, but a public good and a right.	2010 http://periodismohumano.com/
La Marea	For us, journalism means sitting in front of the computer with no political or corporate pressure influencing what we write. It means, for example, being able to publish the name of a bank responsible for evictions without worrying that they will withdraw their advertising. This is the only journalism we believe in. We are committed to investigative journalism and analysis. Our aim is to provide information with no ties to business or political interests.	2012 www.lamarea.com/
Cuartopoder	One value that has disappeared is the function of the press as a counterpower. Indeed, *Contrapoder* (Counterpower) was one of the names for the newspaper and passionately defended by some. The final choice was *Cuartopoder* (fourth power) because it seemed to best summarise our commitment to classical journalism understood originally as a counterpower. We believe we are able to show, paraphrasing the alter-globalisation slogan, that another journalism is possible, one that goes beyond the large communication and entertainment conglomerates.	2010 www.cuartopoder.es
porCausa	*porCausa* promotes research and journalism projects on poverty and inequality. We are committed to public service journalism backed by multidisciplinary data and teams. Our funding comes from private donations.	2013 http://porcausa.org

The second form of alternative journalism that also performs a monitoring function is citizen journalism. Anonymous individuals can become news producers and distributors through Web 2.0 platforms and social media (Allan & Thorsen 2009). They can spread messages, images and information on topics of interest through blogs, social network sites such as Facebook, microblogging services such as Twitter (Murthy 2011), social video portals such as YouTube and image hosting websites such as Flickr. This paves the way for a potential scenario filled with a polyphony of voices and numerous information actors.

With digital technologies, anybody can disseminate information denouncing the abuses, malpractice and injustices of political and economic powers through user-generated content. This type of news circulation can also lead to civic monitoring by bringing to light issues or injustices hidden from public view. Citizen journalism may, therefore, encourage people to participate politically through mobilising and activism (Harlow 2012).

In the Spanish context, one of the main contributions of citizen journalism to civic monitoring of the centres of power has focused on disseminating social protest, especially by denouncing abuse of power by the police against demonstrators. One illustration of the crucial role this type of journalism can play is the *Primavera Valenciana*, or Valencian Spring (López García 2014). In February 2012, a group of 40 students at Valencia's Luis Vives Secondary School blocked one of the city's main streets to protest against the cuts and the falling standards of public education. Their actions provoked a disproportionate police response complete with high levels of violence and the arrest of one student. This incident triggered a week of protests, demonstrations and police charges.

The social networks were crucial in quickly bringing social actors from other sectors into what originally had begun in the education sector (López García 2014). Social media spread news of the protests and allowed the activists and citizens involved to inform directly and denounce the police abuses, through photographs and videos on digital platforms. The dissemination of the images of police brutality and repression turned the case into a social phenomenon of protest that raised levels of indignation among many citizens outside the field of education. Some of the information and audiovisual material was later used by the mainstream media in their own coverage of the event. The *Levante-EMV* newspaper, for example, invited the public to send in photographs of the demonstrations to the paper's website gallery. With the hashtag #PrimaveraValenciana, the demonstrators, many of them young and intense social network users, instigated a civic monitoring initiative.

Also of note is the Spanish citizen-activist network that evolved to denounce police brutality or other abuses of their power and to spread information about social protests through the social media. This network goes back to 15M, but their actions continue today. Known as 'streamers', from the use of video in internet streaming, they use software and digital devices, especially mobile phones, to transmit video and audio recordings of activist and social movement activity on social networks (Pérez Rioja 2014). These media activists combine testimony, defence of a cause and citizen journalism using channels like Twitter, Facebook, Bambuser and YouTube (Tufekci 2013). They are both producers and consumers of information, setting themselves up as active 'prosumers' and broadcasters of content. As citizen journalists, they provide first-person, eyewitness accounts of evictions, bank sit-ins and other grassroots demonstrations. In particular, they record incidences of police brutality, following the rationale of civic monitoring of abuse of power. Videos documenting, publicising and denouncing such events can bring together up to 30,000 people and subsequently attract large audiences on YouTube. The fame these streamers have acquired has turned them into 'networked microcelebrities' (Tufekci 2013).

Streamers seek to disseminate information linked to activism and social mobilisation that goes beyond the media's agenda, while acting as vigilantes to monitor centres of power (Pérez Rioja 2014). Through their presence on social networks, the images become a means of denouncing, mobilising more citizens, protecting activists and sometimes being used as evidence in court. They have occasionally penetrated the media's agenda, becoming news stories themselves and expanding the range of issues present in the public debate. Their activity, with audiovisual information as their main channel of expression, has often triggered civic monitoring processes.

Streamers appeared in Spain with 15M, but their scope and activity goes beyond the 15M movement. This can be seen in the network of Spanish streamers, Peoplewitness,[12] created in November 2011. These streamers record and broadcast news items of political and social interest, using digital tools and social networks. Some of their reports have attracted the attention of news media, such as *Periodismo Humano*, *El País* and *The Guardian*, gaining access to the news agendas. Other notable individuals working in a similar way in Spain are @mainouv, @alitwitt and @Suysulucha. Pérez Rioja (2014) estimates that there are currently some 66 active streamers in Spain. One of their most recent actions was to cover protests of the *Ley de Seguridad Ciudadana* (Citizen Security Law), also known as the *Ley Mordaza* (Gag Law), which came into force at the beginning of July 2015. Just days afterwards, a group of some 30 people, organised through Facebook, set up camp in Madrid's Puerta del Sol to demand its repeal. After 17 days in the square, on 25 July, the police cleared the *Acampada Mordaza*. The police behaviour was filmed and uploaded onto YouTube.[13] The streamers' intervention led one of Spain's leading newspapers, *El Mundo*, to publish the eviction story,[14] bringing to light a protest that would otherwise have gone unnoticed in the mainstream media. Over the following days, they continued to report the movements, assemblies and activities of the demonstrators on social networks, especially Twitter, gaining visibility in the digital environment.

Despite their potential for extending the range of issues covered on the public agenda and for breaking the news monopoly of the elites, the current information landscape remains in the hands of the mainstream media. They are the gatekeepers controlling the social visibility and the appearance of social actors, their power to speak and their power to present themselves to others (Silverstone 2007). Despite the new alternative journalism platforms, the mainstream media still hold the key that opens up public debate and political discourse to the political demands of civil society (Bakardjieva 2012).[15] Social movements sometimes tailor their information dissemination strategies to attract the attention of the mainstream media, which reproduce and echo their denouncements or political proposals (Casero-Ripollés & Feenstra 2012). This question is explored in greater depth in Chapter 4.

Extending representation beyond parliament

The last form of civic monitoring aims to channel the representation of civil society, especially of minorities, beyond the parliamentary debate, extending the borders of traditional political representation established in the political parties. Civil society is calling for recognition as a political actor capable of influencing political dynamics and decision-making processes beyond voting in the elections.

This type of monitoring encourages the proliferation of non-elected representatives defending specific interests and issues. It implies replacing the basic representative principle of 'one person, one vote, one representative' with a new principle of 'one person, many interests, many voices, multiple votes, multiple representatives' (Keane 2009). The growing number of political demands is matched by a parallel growth in the number of actors coming forward to defend them.

The civil society actors undertaking this type of monitoring may be individuals or groups. They tend to follow similar political agendas, generally focusing on demands for democratic regeneration and criticising the establishment and the political class. Their goal is to influence the political system, and they demand reforms to bring about a more open, transparent democratic system; calls for 'real democracy' are frequently heard. Monitoring in these conditions involves both defending the interests of citizens forgotten by the main political parties and scrutinising the activities of centres of power. Abuse is publically denounced: for example, political corruption, excessive privileges for the political class, the lack of effective channels for citizen participation, the lack of information transparency, media manipulation and the intrusion of economic lobbies in politics. As well as preparing and publicising their proposals, this type of monitoring also involves careful observation of the political decision-making process in government and parliament. Shortcomings are identified in the process whenever necessary.

Citizen movements like 15M and Occupy Wall Street have been instrumental in extending representation beyond parliaments. These citizen groups are characterised, in part, by their use of digital technologies 'to challenge or alter dominant, expected, or accepted ways of doing society, culture, and politics' (Lievrouw 2011, pp. 178–179). They are also non-partisan, non-violent, organised in networks and are distinguished by their intensive use of the internet and social media. These political actors take full advantage of the internet's potential for organising and coordinating, primarily through social networks, large groups quickly and cheaply. Technology, therefore, enables citizens with common interests to interconnect and promote new forms of activism and political participation (Harlow 2012).

In Chapter 1 we saw how the mass demonstrations triggered by 15M in 2011, as a general criticism of the establishment and imbalances in the political system, have given way to myriad direct action initiatives. These initiatives are aimed at tackling specific problems and denouncing abuse of power in areas such as mortgage law, preference shares and spending cuts in health and education. Since 2011, many groups have grown in strength – for example, the *Plataforma de Afectados por la Hipoteca* (PAH), a platform of people affected by mortgages, set up in Barcelona in 2009. New initiatives have sprung up all over Spain: the *Plataforma de Afectados por las Participaciones Preferentes* (Platform of People Affected by Preference Shares); the *Plataforma en Defensa de la Enseñanza Pública* (Platform to Defend Public Education); the *Plataforma Anti-Fracking* (Anti-Fracking Platform); and the *iai@flautas*. [16]

Of these groups, the PAH has already been noted as a significant example of an activist group with a wide political repertoire: stopping evictions, citizen legislative initiatives, *escraches* and bank sit-ins. Parts of the mortgage law, certain banking activities and politicians' failure to act have been successfully scrutinised and denounced. This type of citizen platform mobilisation has spread into practically every aspect of public life affected by public spending cuts. Housing, public health, public education, the environment and state pensions are some of the concerns that have spurred initiatives to scrutinise government measures. Questions about who decides who gets what, when and why are constantly being asked in citizen platforms; they have become unelected representatives but specialists in specific areas and custodians of certain rights.

Platforms set up to defend public health care have had significant success in recent years. In September 2013, the *Marea Blanca* (White Tide), in defence of the public health sector, halted the privatisation of six hospitals in the region of Madrid. The Madrid High Court of Justice suspended the process as a cautionary measure due to possible irregularities in the contracts. The *Asociación de Facultativos Especialistas de Madrid* (AFEM), the Association of Medical Specialists in Madrid, one of the most active groups in the *Marea Blanca*, played a crucial role in bringing this case to court. Their organisation and collaboration with legal experts helped to stop this privatisation and drew attention to malpractice throughout the tendering process. Other platforms include the *Plataforma en Defensa de la Enseñanza Pública* that carefully analyses education spending cuts and the problems arising from them; the *Plataforma Anti-Fracking* assesses and denounces the environmental risks associated with hydraulic fracturing; and the *Plataforma Afectados por las Participaciones Preferentes* is organised to take legal action against banks that used unethical practices to sell toxic financial products. Activist groups like *iai@flautas* support a range of platforms and initiatives as well as denouncing wasteful local and regional government spending on numerous megaprojects.

All these platforms combine organisation through the internet and street demonstrations. They use digital technologies to contact their supporters, draw up their manifestos and organise their activities. Of the many different applications of new communication tools, online petitions are one of the most widespread strategies of online participation (Earl & Kimport 2011). These petitions are an innovative and accessible way of monitoring. They can be understood as an extension of representation beyond the parliamentary system, promoting campaigns on a wide range of demands by collecting signatures as a kind of digital vote. Prominent digital platforms for citizens' concerns and demands include ThePetitionSite, Change.org and Avaaz. They use the internet to mount low-cost campaigns and host connections to a wide range of digital tools such as websites, blogs, social networks and emails with which to rapidly spread their petitions. Examples abound of how these digital voting tools have been used. Some have enjoyed great success in both the number of signatures they collect and their penetration of public debate. One notable Spanish case was a petition calling for a tick box in the income tax declaration form where taxpayers would be able to allocate part of their taxes to science.[17] This initiative gathered over 269,000 digital signatures and was taken to parliament by the Plural Left parliamentary group.[18] Although the proposal was not approved, the campaign sparked widespread debate on the lack of funding for research. Another petition collected 150,000 signatures on Change.org calling for the elimination of accommodation expenses for members of parliament for their own residences in Madrid.[19]

Online petition platforms strengthen the voice of civil society by providing new tools to pressurise and legitimise the demands made of the political system. Furthermore, demands that 'go viral' are more likely to be included on the media agenda, increasing their chances of gathering more signatures. The online petition platform is yet another tool that can extend the range of the voices and issues in the public sphere.

Conclusions

The political context in Spain can in no way be described as apathetic and inactive as a result of a post-democratic drift (Crouch 2004); indeed, it may be considered as an exceptional political testing ground. Although Spain shares symptoms of apathy with many other countries, such as declining numbers of political party members, discontent with the political class and disaffection with electoral processes, the Spanish political context is unique in its wealth of incessant democratic experiments spawned by the political and economic crisis. Politics has become part of everyday life and is expressed through numerous dynamic forces. Distrust of the main parties has not combined with the economic crisis to produce a crisis of legitimacy and acceptance of the democratic system. Quite the contrary, numerous civil society spaces are calling for *more democracy* (Haro Barba & Sampedro 2011). Public scrutiny is now an important factor in revealing the failings of the political and economic system. The aspiration of greater democratisation and transparency in public institutions underlies public scrutiny.

Citizen response to the political crisis in Spain does not seem to tally with the minimalist theoretical interpretations of democracy. The 'circulation of elites', as described by Schumpeter (2003, p. 269), does not explain citizens' predilection for active involvement in political life. The work of alternative and independent media, direct action platforms, collective monitoring platforms and the new political parties all share one central feature: the purpose of their actions is to shine light into the dark corners of power. This objective is greatly aided by the political potential of the new digital communication tools.

The digital environment offers citizens new possibilities for participating in politics, not least in the way the monitoring processes are encouraged. Such processes are linked to the concept of monitory democracy carried out by agents, mostly from civil society. They scrutinise the centres of power, closely observe how public resources are managed or how political and economic decisions are made, and publicly denounce cases in which something goes wrong. The presence of these actors and dynamics signals an important new direction.

Digital technologies have the capacity to make monitoring possible and to promote it. As such, these technologies are emerging as an instrumental infrastructure in the monitory process. Communication is also essential to public monitoring, since many of its processes are based on disseminating information (usually secret, alternative or excluded) to achieve their scrutinising goals. Internet and social media now provide autonomous spaces where citizens can instigate public scrutiny, which is understood as a manifestation of political activism. In this vein, monitoring is a kind of counterpower that aims to challenge the centres of political and economic power.

Monitoring has gained new strength in today's societies due to the increasing embeddedness of the digital environment. Monitoring processes have grown and spread and are increasingly diverse and complex. Monitoring processes are now a key form of political participation in the digital era, especially in contexts affected by disillusionment and the crisis of politics. The proliferation of scandals, leaked information and collaborative scrutiny processes reveal how the theoretical monitory democracy framework can be useful in understanding some of the essential dynamics appearing in Spain's complex political landscape. It remains to be seen whether these initiatives will lead to the consolidation of a predominantly transparent democracy in the future or whether the passing of time, and the machinations of the centres of power, will eventually silence these critical voices. What seems clear for the moment is that the political laboratory is also growing in terms of the processes of participation taking root in Spanish civil society.

Notes

1 http://quehacenlosdiputados.net/que-es-que-hacen/.
2 The MySociety.org initiative was launched in the United Kingdom with the conviction that 'intense accountability and active civil society are essential

to the common welfare'. MySociety emerged from the UK Citizens Online Democracy project and currently aggregates many websites, including FixMyTransport, WriteToThem and FixMyStreet, each of which specialises in some function of public scrutiny or online citizen participation. Among these is the website TheyWorkForYou, which provides detailed information about British Members of Parliament, including how many times they have voted, their interventions, the committees on which they work, their attendance and biographies.

3   www.civio.es/medios-2/.
4   http://15mparato.wordpress.com/.
5   Other notable examples of parliamentary monitoring and scrutiny by citizen platforms or independent associations in other countries include VoteWatch.eu (European Parliament) and Openaustralia.org (Australia).
6   https://wikileaks.org/About.html.
7   https://filtrala.org/.
8   http://xnet-x.net/buzonx.
9   Current URL of the blog (in Italian): http://odiolacasta.blogspot.it/.
10   In February 2015, 140 journalists from 45 countries collaborated to publish this list. The information, offered exclusively in Spain by LaSexta and *El Confidencial*, is available at: www.elconfidencial.com/tags/temas/lista-falciani-14093/ and www.lasexta.com/noticias/economia/total-140-periodistas-paises-participan-publicacion-lista-falciani_2015020900194.html.
11   Falciani has also taken part in *Partido X's* anti-corruption committee and is working with *Podemos* to prepare a report on methods of combating fraud.
12   http://peoplewitness.net.
13   Ver: www.youtube.com/watch?t=32&v=aP03BWkUQBQ.
14   Ver: www.elmundo.es/madrid/2015/07/25/55b403da46163fc4388b457d.html.
15   The mainstream media have also played the monitoring role in some recent cases. The work of the press (especially *El País* and *El Mundo*) in reporting on *Partido Popular* funding and the 'Bárcenas Papers' and the TV programmes *Salvados* (La Sexta), *Olvidados* and *Zaida Cantera* are some notable examples.
16   Particularly noteworthy are http://afectadosporlahipoteca.com;http://www.plataforma-afectados-participaciones-preferentes.es and www.iaioflautas.org/.
17   The proposal was first made in a post by a young scientist Francisco J. Hernández on http://resistencianumantina.blogspot.com.es/2012/01/casilla-de-apoyo-la-ciencia-en-la.html.
18   www.change.org/p/casilla-de-apoyo-a-la-ciencia-en-la-declaraci%C3%B3n-de-la-renta-0-7.
19   www.change.org/p/congreso-de-los-diputados-anulen-dietas-de-alojamiento-a-diputados-con-casa-en-madrid.

4 Two-way street mediatisation of politics or overturn? The social media communication models of 15M and *Podemos*

Since 2011, Spain has also become a testing ground for innovation in the field of political communication and is giving rise to some interesting contributions for reshaping democracy. This is mainly due to the emergence of the 15M movement, which has brought about political and social transformations and has had a considerable impact in the field of communication. Indeed, this movement may be regarded as the spearhead of numerous changes in communication logics and strategies used in the political area. We argue that 15M spawned two highly innovative communication models, which, despite having come from the same source, have different approaches, functional logics and embodiments. In both cases, social media are now an essential mechanism for communicating politics and generating new democratic potential.

To understand the extent of this innovation, the present context of political communication must be considered. Although this context is marked by the new social networks sites and digital media, this has not led to the disappearance or decline of the traditional mainstream media (i.e. press, radio and television); they continue to occupy a preferential position (McNair 2006; Blumler & Coleman 2015). This parallel existence is creating a highly hybridised and complex context in which old and new logics are combined (Chadwick 2013).

The aim of this chapter is to analyse the bases and articulation of the two communication models to come out of 15M. One is linked to online political activism, corresponding to the first phase of the 15M movement. The other is associated with *Podemos*, the political party created in January 2014 that is closely linked to the *indignados*. As well as their shared origins, the protagonists in these two cases are political actors from outside the institutional political system – from the periphery – and are associated with activism and social movements. Our interest in analysing them lies in the innovative nature of both models, which determines their potential to transform the current dynamics and practices of political communication, and their potential to generate changes in democracy.

To meet this objective, we first describe the current situation in the field of political communication, which is characterised by the growing role of social media and the continuing predominance of the mainstream media. First we review the effects of digital technologies on political organisation, mobilisation and communication. Two case studies are then analysed through the lens of communication. From this premise, the two models arising from 15M are examined in light of their communication strategies: The first is linked to online political activism, and the second, *Podemos*. We conclude by presenting aspects they have in common and the innovations they introduce into political communication, particularly their contributions to democracy. The analysis is based on a combination of case study methodology and in-depth interviews.

Social media and mainstream media in today's political communication

The impact of social media on politics: organisation, mobilisation and communication

Social media have introduced numerous transformations to political communication that have the potential to impact democracy (Loader & Mercea 2012). They can be seen especially among actors involved in social movements, such as political activists, who are more receptive to innovations in communication. The approaches and attitudes towards communication from traditional political actors are much more conservative (Blumler & Coleman 2015; Lilleker & Vedel 2013). Digital technologies particularly affect three key dimensions of political action: organisation, mobilisation and communication. They contribute to shaping and conditioning these dimensions by introducing changes in the way they function.

In the organisational dimension, social media facilitate the creation of communities of people with shared common interests and encourage more direct relationships among political actors and their supporters. Coordination becomes faster, more streamlined and effective. Digital platforms used for organisational purposes can shape the structure and functioning of political bodies and actors. In cases such as 15M political activists, who make intensive use of these technologies, it is particularly evident (Anduiza, Cristancho & Sabucedo 2014). These social movements regard social media as a natural, favourable habitat in which to create and develop their political activity, generating values and codes that shape their own cultural logic (Juris 2008). This affects the way they organise, making them more flexible, decentralised and interconnected through the internet. Organisation is both large scale and personalised, with inclusive and individualised frameworks for action corresponding to the parameters of the logic of connective action (Bennett & Segerberg 2013). Another consequence of using social media is organisational hybridisation (Chadwick 2007). The most institutional political actors – for instance, political parties – adopt ways of working that combine traditional mechanisms with the digital repertoires associated with social movements. This trend is reflected in the case of *Podemos*, whose organisational dynamics combine classic institutional components with mechanisms from activism.

Social media have also brought innovations to political mobilisation. Once again, political activists have been at the forefront of this exploration, with 15M being a clear example (Anduiza, Cristancho & Sabucedo 2014; Sampedro & Lobera 2014; Candón Mena 2013; López García 2012). Digital technologies allow citizens to mobilise quickly, cheaply and efficiently, lowering the costs of participating and creating new incentives for mobilising. The internet not only provides channels for participating in online campaigns on platforms such as Change.org or Avazz.org, but it can also be used to announce demonstrations. This potential was heavily exploited by 15M and its offshoots, such as 25S and *Rodea el Congreso* (Surround Parliament), for coordinating activists to prevent evictions. *Plataforma de Afectados por la Hipoteca* (PAH) also successfully used this tactic intensively. Social media, however, have met criticism for generating weak links and for lowering levels of participant engagement and commitment (Gladwell 2010), leading to armchair activism or 'slacktivism'. This term refers to the way some people lend their support to causes, but with the minimum effort or sacrifice, participating through computers or mobile devices without leaving the comfort of their homes to demonstrate in the streets. Although this gives the armchair activist a feeling of satisfaction, some authors argue it has no political impact and renders the effect of this type of mobilisation insignificant to those in power (Morozov 2011).

Despite what has been mentioned above, social media have helped to overhaul the repertoire of tactics and actions for political mobilisation. These include online petitions, hacktivism (e.g. WikiLeaks, Anonymous), online donations, virtual occupations and boycotts, email campaigns, protest websites and profiles on social networks sites or alternative digital media (Van Laer & Van Aelst 2010). The catalogue of possible actions is also constantly growing precisely because it depends on the creativity of activists who are continually generating innovations and new formulas for political participation (Earl & Kimport 2011).

Social media have introduced a wide range of innovations in the field of communication. They offer new communication platforms with which political actors and activists can publicise their messages and their demands. This is particularly useful and relevant for activists because of the difficulties they face in accessing mainstream media. Twitter plays a key role in disseminating news and information because it bypasses the traditional news creators represented by the mainstream media (Gerbaudo 2012). Connected to this, digital technology enables political actors to produce and disseminate their own content, turning them into communication actors with a wide level of autonomy. This allows them to activate self-mediation processes (Cammaerts 2012) to publicise their own issues and frames. Political activists use these issues and frames to build their own counter-hegemonic and critical narratives that express their interests, give voice to the silenced and play the role of opposition to the dominant elites (Fuchs 2014a). Bound up with the emergence of a new communication modality is mass self-communication consisting of self-produced messages, in which publication is self-directed and reception is self-selected by those participating in the communicative process (Castells 2009). The result is content generated by users who, some argue, are the seed of participatory culture that empowers citizens (Jenkins 2006).

The digital landscape strengthens the key role of communication and its strategic management. Communication strategies are needed if political actors – parties or activists – want to achieve these outcomes: inform citizens, persuade citizens of the actors' view of social issues, participate in public debate, shape the public agenda, promote formed public opinion and influence the process of designing public policies and decision making. The importance of communication strategies in the process of social influence now lies at the heart of politics more than ever before.

Media protagonism and the mediatisation of politics

Despite the growing importance of social media, the mainstream media continue to hold the centre ground in political communication. Their key role as gatekeepers, controlling access to society's awareness of politics, means they have a huge influence in the social construction of political reality. The mainstream media, particularly television, are citizens' main source of political information. The public's image and knowledge of politics is largely conditioned by the representations of events prepared, published, and broadcast by the media.

The media stage is where politics are played out in our society. Media spaces, whether for information or for entertainment, can give high social visibility to political messages, events and candidates. Access to the media opens up channels to reach mass audiences. Political actors, particularly parties, governments and other institutional actors, are constantly cultivating their media relations to attract attention and gain access to the news. The media have a language, a narrative format and modes of production that follow their own rules: media logic (Altheide & Snow 1979). Media logic involves a set of criteria applied in the preparation of news that determines its format and the way citizens perceive politics. Media logic introduces, among other aspects, simplification, personalisation, acceleration, spectacularisation and entertainment in political information (Esser & Matthes 2013).

In order to obtain favourable news coverage and take advantage of the central position of the mainstream media, political actors have no choice but to adapt to the media logic and follow its rules. As a result, they are subject to the media's criteria. Gaining access to political marketing techniques is one of the consequences of adopting the media logic (Lees-Marshment 2011). Political actors design communication strategies that promote candidates as a brand, appealing to emotions and adapting their messages to the preferences of the public and the media.

As well as having their own logic, the media are not a neutral channel for the flow of political information; rather, they are themselves active and significant political actors. The media are guided by their own interests in the news production process and in the social representation of politics. These interests may be either political, defending their ideas and values, or economic, protecting their business and corporate interests. Their status as political actors means they set out to influence other political actors by conditioning their agenda and decision-making processes, and to influence citizens by attempting to shape their opinions and viewpoints.

The dominant role of the mainstream media as political source, actor and stage, and the way political actors adapt to their logic, is known as the mediatisation of politics (Mazzoleni & Schulz 1999). It is a process that activates four interrelated dimensions (Strömbäck 2008). The first dimension identifies the media as the primary source of political information. The second denotes that they are clearly independent of the political system. The third confirms that political news content is controlled by the media logic with minimum interference from political actors in its preparation. Finally, the fourth dimension states that political actors adapt to media rules and bend to the control of the media logic. Mediatisation portrays a landscape where the media have a huge influence on politics, where they play a leading role as political actors defending their own values and interests, and where they play a key role in articulating the public's political knowledge. Mediatisation, therefore, emerges as a highly influential theoretical approach to explain the workings of political communication over recent decades (Strömbäck & Esser 2014).

Some critical authors argue that mediatisation is a poorly defined concept not only because of the variety and diversity of approaches taken to it but also because it has become a deposit for diverse theoretical perspectives (Deacon & Stanyer 2014). Lunt & Livingstone (2016) see mediatisation as a concept in the general sense of a reference and guide, suggesting it would be difficult to apply empirically. The main criticism lies in its media-centric viewpoint, given that the mainstream media are afforded the foremost role as catalysts for social change while the roles of non-media factors are downplayed (Deacon & Stanyer 2014). The media are understood as extraordinarily powerful institutions with far-reaching effects on all types of political and social practices. Media influence is considered to go in one direction only: out to other social spheres. According to mediatisation theory, therefore, the central functions of politics depend on the media (Mazzoleni & Schulz 1999). This contention generates the negative view of the media as having a perverse influence on politics (Livingstone 2009).

Mediatisation assumes that political actors have no choice but to adapt to the media's rules and criteria (Strömbäck 2008) if they want to avoid social invisibility. Deacon & Stanyer (2014), however, argue that other reactions and responses are possible. Another concern is that mediatisation focuses almost exclusively on the classic mainstream media, especially television, and ignores the digital environment (Jensen 2013).

The emergence of social media and the dominant mediatisation of politics have led to a situation in which old and new media coexist – that is, a hybrid environment. In turn, this has generated an interrelationship among platforms and an interdependency among the tools used in political communication strategies. The mainstream media and the digital media constantly interact to create a hybrid media system in which sometimes competitive and sometimes collaborative logics try to influence the flow of information and the social representation of politics (Chadwick 2013). This dynamic may indeed alter the classic dynamics of the mediatisation of politics based on the predominance of the mainstream media.

Parties and candidates have not given up their old communication tactics and tools, but have enriched them by incorporating the new media logics and possibilities from the digital landscape. This has spawned hypermedia campaigns (Howard 2005; Lilleker, Tenscher & Štětka 2015) containing both old and new media logics. Political activists are aware of this situation and use and produce a genuine mixture of media and mediations for conveying their demands and spreading their protests: from alternative digital media, through mainstream media, to social media. This was implemented by 15M (Micó & Casero-Ripollés 2014) using their own non-commercial social networks (e.g. Diaspora*, Occupii, *N-1*) as well as commercial social media (e.g. Facebook and Twitter). The former was used for internal communication and to coordinate the protests, and the latter, widely used among activists, to disseminate and extend their demands and to win new support (Fuchs 2014b).

The political actors' relationship with the mainstream media takes diverse forms. Institutional actors – such as governments, political parties and trade unions – predominantly adapt to the media logic and mediatisation (Strömbäck & Esser 2014). Social movements, in contrast, have a wider range of choice. Rucht (2004) proposes four main options, which he terms the 'quadruple A'. The first is 'abstention'. Born out of frustration with negative, or a lack of, media coverage, abstention involves rejecting any relations with the media. The second is 'attack', which consists of orchestrating campaigns to challenge bias and a lack of neutrality in the mass media. The third is the 'creation of "alternative" digital media' to broadcast a different news agenda. Finally, the fourth is 'adaptation', which entails playing by the rules of the mainstream media game in order to attract its attention and appear in the news.

The 15M communication model: the relationship between online political activism and the mainstream media

The first communication model, with its roots in 15M, is that of activists from the movement's initial stages involving the *acampadas* in public spaces, particularly the Plaza del Sol in Madrid and the Plaza Catalunya in Barcelona. This model was limited to the first moments of 15M. As the movement developed, changes were introduced to this initial format. Its initial contribution was innovative in the way it attempted to establish a new pattern of relations among political activists and the mainstream media and journalists. This was a completely original and unprecedented strategy in political communication. More than just anecdotal, this experience was especially relevant because of its impact on highly technologicalised social movements in other parts of the world, such as Occupy in London and New York. It was adopted by online political activists as a reference model and, because of its example for other political and civic organisations, as a way to establish relations with the mainstream media in the future.

Between hostility and alternative digital media

Relations between social movements and the mainstream media and journalists have traditionally been fraught (McCurdy 2012). Activists have regarded the mass media with hostility and mistrust for three reasons. The first is related to political activists' understanding of the mainstream media as fundamental to maintaining and perpetuating capitalism and dominant elites. This view derives from a post-Althusserian perspective that regards the media as an ideological apparatus dominated by state and capitalist interests that are structurally biased against social movements and protests (Cammaerts 2012).

The second reason lies in the news coverage of activists' interventions in the mainstream media that tends to be biased and unfavourable to social movements and protests (Rucht 2004). In general, the 'protest paradigm' (Gitlin 1980; McLeod 2007; Harlow & Johnson 2011) prevails, in which the news focuses on protests as a spectacle, highlighting sensationalist details such as violence, drama and deviant or strange behaviour.

The third reason is related to access to the media; activists often accuse the mainstream media of silencing them and keeping protests off the public agenda by failing to report them (Gamson & Wolfsfeld 1993). In the case of 15M, political activists were deeply mistrustful and critical of the mainstream media. The main newspapers were displayed under the banner '*El rincón de las mentiras*' ('Lies Corner') in a space created in the Plaza del Sol in Madrid, for example.

The natural and traditional reaction to this situation is for political activists to create alternative media and communication spaces (Downing 2001). Alternative media combine two features: grassroots participation in the communication environment (Atton 2002; Hartley 2009) and critical, counter-hegemonic content produced as an alternative to the mainstream media agendas (Fuchs 2010). Political activists promote and encourage such content in their communication strategies as a form of opposition and resistance (Atton 2002). The case of 15M is no exception.

Two types of alternative media were in evidence in the *indignados* movement. Media was developed by activists during the protest to provide independent communication channels for their messages and activities (Barranquero Carretero & Meda González 2015; Fernández-Planells, Figueras-Maz & Freixa 2014). One of the most notable independent channels was Sol TV. Through real-time internet streaming, events in the Plaza del Sol *acampada* were broadcast using a fixed camera. Another example was Ágora Sol Radio,[1] a digital radio station set up during the occupation to give a voice to the *indignados*. The station still broadcasts today as a kind of assembly aiming to keep alive the spirit of social change of 15M. Toma La Tele[2] is an audio-visual platform launched in March 2012 that broadcasts content from activist groups. The newspaper *Madrid15m* [3] is produced monthly by 15M assemblies in the neighbourhoods of Madrid. Instigated by the *Asamblea Popular de Villaverde*, it is conceived as an alternative source of information focusing on 15M issues. In October 2016, it published its 51st edition.

This strategy is not exclusive to the Spanish experience, and similar initiatives have been set in motion in recent Occupy mobilisations and other events. The protesters in London launched their own alternative media, *The Occupied Times of London*, playing on the name of *The Times*, one of the most traditional and conservative elite newspapers in the United Kingdom. The *Occupied Wall Street Journal* made a similar appearance in New York.

The second types of alternative media, with links to 15M, are independent media. Although not part of the movement, these media are sympathetic to its cause and include 15M issues on their news agenda (Casero-Ripollés & Feenstra 2012). Examples include *Diagonal*, [4] *Directa* [5] and *Periodismo Humano*, [6] which broadcast live from the camp in Madrid. Particularly notable is *Madrilonia*, [7] a blog linked to the Metropolitan Observatory of Madrid and closely associated with 15M's demands.

Despite the advantages the digital context and social media offer for creating alternative media by increasing public access to free expression (Shirky 2011), they are still insufficient to give political activism social visibility, guarantee wide dissemination of their demands or achieve real success. The online activists interviewed for this book, as well as those in other countries (Harlow & Harp 2013), state that alternative media face serious difficulties in getting their information out beyond activist circles. In consequence, they see the mainstream media as an essential mechanism for conveying their demands to a wider public and recognise that they must reconsider their relationship with the mainstream media players.

Overturning the media logic

In examining 15M's model of relations with the mainstream media, it becomes clear that the movement is at a crossroads. 15M activists were fully convinced of the importance of communication and the mainstream media to gain public visibility and to spread their demands to other sectors of society. This removed any possibility of opting for the first of Rucht's (2004) 'A's – abstention, or refusing to deal with the media. At the same time, they were aware that alternative digital media aligned to their cause were insufficient to meet this objective. Opting only for the 'A' for alternative would be a partial strategy. Accepting the media logic and opting for Rucht's (2004) adaptation model, however, would generate huge debate and deep tensions among 15M political activists. They were already mistrustful of the mainstream media and took different and sometimes opposing sides.

Faced with this dilemma, the 15M activists' response was to establish a new frame of relations with the media in an attempt to have an influence by conditioning the news coverage of the movement. This was possible through social media and the digital environment, which the activists saw as an alternative playing field to that of the mainstream media. It was in this setting that a new, highly innovative strategy for dealing with the media came about: the overturn of media logic.

The strategy involved breaking away from news management principles based on public relations and avoiding the rules of the mediatisation of politics, but without rejecting relations with the mainstream media. This approach had various dimensions with various practical consequences, the first of which was to do with personalisation. The 15M political activists had no permanent spokespersons for dealing with the media, either formally or informally, and had no leaders that the media could identify and personalise. Journalists tasked with covering 15M news complained that an ad hoc spokesperson they dealt with one day would not answer their phone calls and requests on the following day (Micó & Casero-Ripollés 2014). The absence of a valid, constant news source generated uncertainty among the journalists by disrupting their ingrained routines and their need for easily accessible and available sources.

The 15M activists wanted to speak for the entire protest as a single group (Candón Mena 2013). For this reason, no permanent spokespersons were appointed, preventing the media from personalising the message of the protests by focusing on one individual or a small group of people. This collective voice joined the chorus of individual voices of the participants in the protests to feed into and shape the collective response. A 'multitudinous identity' (Monterde et al. 2015) was activated, marked by social transversality, internal heterogeneity and distributed leadership.

The second practical effect of the overturn of media logic affected formal issues, since the 15M activists avoided conventional mechanisms in their dealings with the mainstream media. They held very few press conferences, had little personal contact with journalists and issued no supplementary information such as press releases. This was not due to their rejection of the media, their underestimation of the importance of communication, or their disorganisation. Indeed, the opposite was true: 15M activists set up communication committees to prepare news information about their cause that they published through numerous information channels, principally social networks (Micó & Casero-Ripollés 2014; Fuchs 2014b). As noted previously, they also created their own alternative digital media, Sol TV and Ágora Sol Radio. Members of the communication committees were skilled in the area of communication. Many were journalists themselves with a thorough knowledge of the professional workings and dynamics of mainstream journalism.

The third element in the overturn of media logic is related to dispersion. The 15M political activists did not have a unified, centralised message. This was due in part to the wide range of issues on their political agenda (Casas, Davesa & Congosto 2016), the transversal nature of the movement and its links with a more personalised political action that is by nature more heterogeneous (Bennett & Segerberg 2013). The fact that they moved among many different issues and arenas went against the media logic's requirements for a simplified message that would fit into the limited space and time available to produce and disseminate the news. For example, 15M spawned a huge constellation of websites, blogs and profiles on social media due to the movement's open, decentralised and assembly-based nature as well as its multitudinous identity that encouraged the free expression of ideas and debate. This diffusion was criticised by some journalists in terms of communication efficiency and for its separation and dispersion of materials and resources (Micó & Casero-Ripollés 2014). Once again, this baffled the journalists, who did not know what the movement's 'official' position was. They were disorientated in the midst of such a broad political agenda, and they frequently met with contradictions in the discourses of the activists, without knowing which ones to accept. The journalists reporting on the 15M found this context extremely complex to work within.

The fourth and final dimension of the overturn of media logic concerns displacement. The 15M political activists wanted to move media relations into the digital platforms of the social media. These platforms were regarded as an information channel and as a vital practical environment in which activism was created and developed (Haro-Barba & Sampedro 2011; López García 2012). The social networks constitute a 'cultural logic of networking' (Juris 2008), encompassing all the values, codes and actions of activism. By shifting the relationship with the mainstream media to social media, the activists dislodged the journalists from their cultural logic and their working routines. This brought the journalists onto 15M's home ground; the activists were confident that they would now be at an advantage in their dealings with the media. Social media became indispensable to political activists' subversion of the media logic.

Through this communication strategy, the 15M activists refused to adapt to the criteria imposed by the media logic and set out to make the journalists adopt their rules. Unlike other political actors such as governments, political parties or trade unions, which adapt to the established media parameters (Strömbäck & Esser 2014), 15M activists set their own rules for media relations. This was unprecedented in the field of political communication strategies and created a new model. The activist logic thus emerged to confront the media logic head on. The activist logic questions the rules and criteria imposed by the media in political news coverage, but it does not rule out relationships with them. In other words, it challenges the mediatisation of politics but not the central role of the media in the field of political communication.

The aim of this logic is to promote a new, more open and flexible dynamic to shape the public agenda – a way for political activists to convey issues and frames to a wider audience. It seeks to incorporate the demands of political activists into public debate and potentially become involved in the public policy-making and decision-making processes controlled by the political system.

Turning around how the public agenda is set

One of the central tenets of activist logic and the overturn of media logic put into practice by the 15M activists was to turn around the way the agenda was set. Through the strategic use of social media, they attempted to get their demands and discourses on the media agenda by influencing news content. In doing so, they aspired to use the mainstream media as unwitting loudspeakers to amplify the reach and circulation of their demands. This strategy was based on highly organised digital campaigns, mainly on Twitter but also on Facebook, to generate trending topics, thereby attracting media attention. The 15M activists used a range of digital tools to this end: email lists, pads (collaborative documents similar to a digital notepad created with applications such as Titanpad) and the social media. The first two were used to organise and mobilise activists, and the third was used as an information channel.

These 15M digital campaigns centred on two key aspects: creating a hashtag to identify an issue and to generate a frame, and synchronising thousands of participants to simultaneously spread messages with that hashtag. This second strategy required high levels of calculation and coordination in order to mobilise thousands of activists at exactly the same time. According to the political activists interviewed, the success of this strategy depended on the movement's strong network of users and profiles. This type of intervention showed that self-organisation and coordination on the one hand, and following the concept of multiple intelligences (Lévy 2001), solidarity and cooperation on the other, are vital ingredients in launching new dynamics for building the public agenda in the social media.

Both the issue and substance of the campaign, as well as the exploitation of the political opportunity (Meyer & Minkoff 2004) and the media structure (Cammaerts 2012), are also essential. The demands of the 15M political agenda are clearly tied in with the central factors of Spain's political climate. The political climate was heavily characterised by the injustices and negative effects of the economic crisis on the majority of the population, contrasting with the privileges and irresponsibility of the political and economic elites. Some of the hashtags that became trending topics were from before the *acampadas*, such as *#nolesvotes* ('don't vote for them') and *#democraciarealya* ('real democracy now'). Some were used during the occupations, such as *#spanishrevolution*, *#tomalaplaza* ('take the square') and *#nonosvamos* ('we're not leaving'). Others were from subsequent actions, such as *#stopdesahucios* ('stop evictions'), *#rodeaelcongreso* ('surround parliament') and *#corruPPlandia* (a play on the word 'corruption' and the initials of the *Partido Popular*).

These digital campaigns, for which 15M activists prepared several instruction manuals,[8] sought to set the agenda through a bottom-up process by influencing the mainstream media to include the activists' demands in their news content. This strategy placed the social media at the heart of the 15M communication policy and revealed the activists' technological proficiency and expertise, as well as their communication skills, which enabled them to exploit the workings of the media system to their advantage.

The most significant illustration of this bottom-up agenda in the Spanish context is the case of the *Plataforma de Afectados por la Hipoteca* (PAH). This citizen platform campaigns for the right to decent housing and against evictions, and used its actions and campaigns to get its demands first on the media agenda and then on the public agenda (Alonso-Muñoz & Casero-Ripollés 2016). The question of assets in lieu of payment – that is, when a person threatened with eviction hands their property over to the bank and their mortgage is cancelled – was brought into Spanish public debate. This issue had previously been absent from mainstream media news content and the political parties' priorities. Through their mobilisations and their handling of communication on social networks and Web 2.0, the PAH has brought to light one of the greatest social consequences of the economic crisis, previously silenced: the trauma of eviction and the injustices of the mortgage law.

The 15M activists, promoted by the social media, sought to influence the content of the media agenda using this framework. They considered that by adopting this formula they could influence the news selection process and the modus operandi of the mainstream media. This scenario had two substantial effects on political communication. First, activists, and with them the public, abandoned the passive role that consigned them to the media and political peripheries and began proactively and autonomously setting their own agendas in the social media environment (Kim & Lee 2007). Second, the mainstream media and political actors lost their monopoly over decisions as to what makes it into the news. This opened up the process of constructing the public agenda to new social actors, like political activists, as in the case of 15M in Spain. Although the objective of the bottom-up agenda is to influence the media agenda, the mainstream media continue to play a central role in managing the public agenda and controlling visibility of political affairs at the social level. The mainstream media, both on- and offline, still hold control over the public's attention on the news and in political affairs (Hindman 2009).

Podemos's communication model: taking on the media without abandoning the networks

The second communication model deriving from 15M is that of *Podemos*, the political party founded in January 2014 with links to the *indignados* movement. In this section, we will see how the party's communication strategy favours accessing the mainstream media, especially television and political debate programmes, but without giving up its intense activity on social media. This hybrid formula creates a synergy between factors from old and new media and introduces innovative elements into the field of political communication. One of the main elements concerns the role of communication in political action and dynamics. In this case, as in the previous section, we limit our analysis to the initial stage of this model: from the party's foundation in January 2014 to the European elections in May of the same year, when *Podemos* had its first taste of institutional representation, winning five seats in the European Parliament. Our interest focuses on the original conception of *Podemos*, with the aim of measuring its degree of innovation, the changes brought to political communication and its impact on democracy.

Communication: the backbone of the Podemos political project

Many analysts agree that *Podemos*'s electoral success is difficult to separate from its communication strategy – the backbone of its project (Postill 2015; Sampedro 2015). This new party has contributed several innovations to political communication. Unlike the traditional political parties, which understand communication as an instrumental stage at the end of the decision-making process, for *Podemos* communication is the starting point and lies at the heart of its political strategy. From the start, communication is integral to the party's political projects and political activities. This innovation is significant not only in the Spanish context but also on an international scale.

The approach may largely be explained by *Podemos*'s conception of politics, which is based on discourse theory and the importance of hegemony (Howarth 2005; Errejón 2011). This neo-Gramscian perspective holds that political activity is the struggle to construct public meaning. It accepts that social and political events are framed by certain discourses or practices in the production of meaning. Discourse is capable of generating a hegemonic meaning that establishes legitimacy and the public's social support for political proposals, parties and leaders. Those who control and establish the discourse control the political power.

This constructivist approach, following the theories of Laclau (1990, 2005) and Mouffe (1995), states that discourse creates political identities constructed by conflicts and opposition between 'us' and 'them', according to Carl Schmitt's friend–enemy distinction. The importance of discourse in constructing identities and imposing hegemony implies that communication is a vitally important strategic tool and places it at the heart of *Podemos*'s political activity. This explains why communication forms the very foundation of its political project and cannot be separated from it. The axiom that politics is a communicative activity, and communication is a political activity, is reflected in this position. The two are intimately and inextricably linked.

Podemos's strategic positioning vis-à-vis the mainstream media

This conception of politics, linked to discourse and hegemony, has a direct influence on *Podemos*'s communication strategy. Although closely linked to 15M in terms of members and demands (Dader 2015; Sampedro 2015), *Podemos* has an original response to the traditional dilemma of social movements' relations with the mainstream media. In contrast to Rucht's (2004) quadruple A of abstention, attack, alternative and adaptation, its course is to reformulate the mediatisation of politics. Unlike 15M's overturn strategy, *Podemos* practices a two-way mediatisation of politics, going beyond the traditional mediatisation process based on the influence of mainstream media on politics.

What is novel about *Podemos*'s approach is that this decision is not coincidental or spontaneous, but organised, calculated and thought out. The approach passes through different phases, from setting up alternative media to moving into the very heart of the media: free-to-air national television. In parallel, this strategy was accompanied by an intense presence on social media platforms to spread the party messages further and, by going viral, become more visible and familiar to the public.

The founders of *Podemos*, the majority of whom were lecturers at the Complutense University of Madrid,[9] have often explained the pivotal value of communication to the political project and the need to adapt it to the media logic. Pablo Iglesias, leader and secretary general of *Podemos*, states that their 'intervention in the media came about after much reflection', and they had been preparing for it for many years through the television programme *La Tuerka* (Rivero 2014, pp. 95–96). Iñigo Errejón, the party's policy secretary and second in command, sees Iglesias's participation in political debates on Spanish television as a key factor in raising their media visibility. It became the most powerful communication tool and a symbolic catalyst of popular expression in the campaign (Errejón 2014).

Podemos's decision to actively participate and intervene in the mainstream media was neither unplanned nor taken lightly; it was part of a deliberate strategy. *Podemos* understands that mainstream media, especially television, are central spaces for citizen socialisation and politicisation in today's society – in accordance with the paradigm of mediatisation. Iglesias summarised this stance, which recognises the core role of television in political action, in a lecture entitled 'The limits of manipulation: Other information is possible'. He concluded that:

> 90% of a political speech is an audiovisual tool, 95% of leadership is an audiovisual tool, 95% of an electoral or political campaign is an audiovisual tool, and 95% of what a political organisation might say is an audiovisual tool.[10]

Podemos's *leap into the mainstream media*

Podemos implemented a two-stage strategy to reformulate the mediatisation of politics. The first stage was to create an alternative political debate programme on a community television channel. One of the main hypotheses of *Podemos*'s communication strategy was that angry voters could be mobilised through the mainstream media and by preparing arguments and discourses that questioned the traditional parties' proposals. Based on this hypothesis, *Podemos* created an alternative television programme as a training ground that would enable them to move into the mainstream media at a later date. By taking this route, *Podemos*'s founding members clearly distanced themselves from Rucht's (2004) strategies of abstention and attack, which are typically followed by traditional social movements. Instead they opted, initially, for the alternative strategy. Even this option, which took shape in the show *La Tuerka* ('The Screw'), applied the media logic.

La Tuerka was first aired in November 2010 and followed the standard political talk show format. The programme was directed and presented by Pablo Iglesias, who would go on to become the party leader. The show was broadcast on alternative media, first on two community television stations in the Madrid region (Tele K and Canal 33), and later on Público TV, where it continues to be streamed on the internet. After each broadcast, the programme was uploaded onto social media, extending its reach to a much wider public (by August 2016 its YouTube channel had 131,840 subscribers). Social media gave *La Tuerka* wide exposure by moving beyond the limited coverage of the small community television stations that broadcast it. The programme is produced on a very low budget and with limited technical and voluntary human resources. Debates cover political and economic questions such as the effects of austerity, the influence of the Catholic Church in Spanish society, the quality of Spanish democracy and police torture. There is a focus on issues that the mainstream media practically ignore or silence. The programme's format has two premises: to seek out controversy and provocative arguments to attract larger audiences, and to return decorum to television debate through respect for other speakers, without the interruptions, insults and shouting frequently present in similar shows on mainstream media.

La Tuerka has a clear, defined political purpose, linked to the left and social movements, as it seeks to modify the discourses and meanings established by the Spanish political elites. *Podemos*'s founders regard the programme as a space where arguments are put forward that can 'hand out ammunition' for the battle to create meaning and political hegemony (Torres Rodríguez 2015). In order to build a counter-hegemony, *Podemos* accepted the hegemonic operating rules of the mainstream media in the belief that television is a key mechanism for creating hegemony. Pablo Iglesias explained this view in a lecture in September 2013:

> We do what a political party should do. We are delivering arguments to do what Gramsci said a party has to do as an organic intellectual: assemble a large number of people who can act as supporters in their workplaces, schools and universities, in the bar, with friends with family. [...] We are doing what a political party should do: producing ideology through the new mechanism of television.[11]

La Tuerka's successful viewing figures, especially in social media, with more than 44.2 million views by August 2016, together with Pablo Iglesias's controversial character, attracted invitations for him to participate in political talk shows on national free-to-air television networks. This heralded the second phase of *Podemos*'s leap into the mainstream media. On 25 April 2013, Iglesias appeared on the political television talk show *El Gato al Agua*, broadcast by the national free-to-air channel Intereconomía.[12] This right-wing talk show brought Iglesias recognition and was decisive in attracting further invitations to appear on commercial channels with larger audiences, such as La Sexta (*La Sexta Noche*) and Cuatro (*Las mañanas de Cuatro*).

Iglesias' contributions in these programmes were backed up by arguments and examples carefully put together by the team (Torreblanca 2015). They were tailored to the media logic as they responded to provocation and attack, resulting in an entertaining delivery,[13] although with a clearly alternative political content. The major Spanish parties and their privileges were criticised and referred to as *la casta* (the political class). He combined verbal aggression with a carefully controlled cool temperament that made him seem integrally hard, yet soft and well-mannered – a demeanour that won him the support of many viewers (Dader 2015). His style also placed him fully within the infotainment format predominant in today's commercial television. The basis of *Podemos*'s communication strategy is to combine a discourse adapted to the media (media-electoral discourse) with one addressed to ordinary people, who are not necessarily interested in or knowledgeable about politics (popular discourse) (Palao Errando 2015a, 2015b).

The controversial figure of Iglesias, his direct messages and his confrontations with conservative commentators all had a positive impact on viewing figures (Sampedro 2015). As a result, the television networks were happy to do business with *Podemos*. Rising viewing figures attracted more advertising revenue, the principal source of funding for free-to-air television companies. For *Podemos* and the television networks, it was a mutually beneficial relationship: The former, especially Iglesias, gained visibility and public recognition; the latter saw their advertising revenue rise. His television appearances were also rebroadcast on social media, further spreading his message and increasing his visibility (Toret 2015; Sampedro 2015).

Podemos *and the mediatisation of politics*

Podemos's communication strategy acknowledges that the media, mainstream and digital, are at the core of political communication (Mazzoleni & Schulz 1999; Strömbäck 2008). The founders of this new political party highlighted the importance of recognising mainstream media as essential to the public's political socialisation. According to Iglesias, '[T]elevision talk shows are much more important than parliamentary debate' (Rivero 2014, p. 98), and television is 'the best political communication tool of the twenty-first century'.[14] *Podemos*'s diagnosis clearly recognises the need to adopt media criteria that enable it to promote its project and give it visibility. The traditional alternative media are insufficient for taking its message outside the minority circles of the movement and its sympathisers. To reach the maximum number of people and to aspire to influence the general public debate by extending the party's discourse to large sectors of society, the leaders of *Podemos* calculated that they would need to use the mainstream media and build a relationship with them from the outset.

Aware of the insufficiencies of digital media already recognised by the 15M movement, *Podemos*'s communication strategy invested heavily in participation in television talk shows as a springboard into the centre of public debate. Iglesias notes this strategy as a lesson for the traditional left, which scorned such spaces, arguing that 'participating in these debates is pointless; it's counter-productive. We'll keep on doing what we've always done, twelve of us just talking among ourselves...' (Rivero 2014, p. 99). The 2014 European election campaign was an opportunity to put into practice the political communication strategy its members had been rehearsing for years (Torreblanca 2015).

In the 2014 election campaign, *Podemos* attracted media attention by applying two main strategies linked to the mediatisation process: 1) simplifying the message and appealing to emotions; and 2) building media-based leadership and promoting Iglesias as an electoral brand.

1) Simplifying the message and appealing to the emotions

During the campaign, *Podemos*'s message was clear, direct and resonated with the critical mass that identified with 15M. The party's strategy focused on identifying those responsible for corruption and the crisis, and the constantly repeated references to *la casta* were central to its discourse. Spain's complex political context, widespread dissatisfaction with the political class and serious concerns about corruption and fraud (Muriel 2014) made this message especially effective; it identified 'us' and 'the people' as opposed to the minority privileged *la casta* or 'political class or establishment'. This is indeed one of *Podemos*'s key communication and political strategies, aiming to replace the traditional left–right ideological distinction with one distinguishing 'those at the top' (the elite) from 'those at the bottom' (ordinary people) (Errejón 2011; Dader 2015).

The founders of *Podemos* defend the importance of translating complex political diagnoses into simple, straightforward concepts and sentences. When preparing for appearances in the mainstream media, they always began with the question, 'Are you going to talk for the left or for the people?'[15] In other words, they always opted for a clearly understandable discourse, rather than a more intellectual delivery, as a way of reaching larger audiences and falling in with the television media logic. Reducing messages to simple, de-intellectualised proposals is also a way to introduce the emotional factor into politics (Dader 2015). It aims to appeal to a social consciousness shared by a broad citizen base, critical of the way Spanish democracy prevents 'real' citizen participation in politics. The negative consequences of austerity measures and the effects of the economic crisis on the majority of the population are denounced.

This strategy also uses emotions as mobilisation mechanisms. The very name of the party, *Podemos* ('We can'), or slogans such as *Sí se puede* ('Yes, it's possible'), which are associated with other social agents such as the PAH, appeal to the emotions and seek to represent those with an affinity for 15M. The European election campaign slogan, 'When did you last feel excited about voting?',[16] echoed the emotions of dissatisfaction with traditional political parties in the complex Spanish political context. Pablo Iglesias identified this question in his lecture "What is a real democracy?", arguing that passion plays a key role in popular empowerment, and in *Podemos* they had attempted to 'generate a device to excite people'.[17]

The party's digital media discourse also used emotion. Of *Podemos*'s Facebook publications during the electoral campaign, 62 per cent had emotional content, mainly positive emotions such as hope or enthusiasm, linked to posts on aspects of the party's ideology or programme (Sampietro & Valera 2015). Iglesias recognised this strategy when he stated that passion plays a key role in popular empowerment processes.

The same theory had previously been put forward in 2013 by Juan Carlos Monedero, another *Podemos* founder from the Complutense University of Madrid. He stated in an interview that 'we cannot bring back alternative thought by nagging alone', we need to 'bring back some excitement'.[18] Rather than specific political proposals, *Podemos* seeks to transmit values linked to emotional and affective factors at a time of crisis and potential social change in order to obtain maximum possible public support (Dader 2015). In this vein, their communication strategy is similar to Barack Obama's 2008 presidential campaign, which was designed to raise hope; it places the excitement of values above political proposals and programmes.

2) Building media-based leadership and promoting Iglesias as an electoral brand

Podemos's success in the 2014 European elections had a lot to do with Pablo Iglesias's personal popularity. The party's use of a political leader figure, a tactic widely discussed in political theory (Robinson & Tormey 2005; Flesher Fominaya 2007), falls in line with its media projection and visibility strategy. On this question, Iglesias stated, 'I think a leader fulfils the same function as an advertising slot, a sticker or a poster […]. It's a political communication tool' (Muriel 2014).

Iglesias's idea of media leadership coincides with that of a good television communicator – a personality that can clearly bring his or her message to the public debate. Leadership is understood in strategic and communication terms and as a mechanism to bring *Podemos*'s politics to larger sections of the electorate. A leader's role is as a catalyst for collective indignation, on the one hand, and as a reference for a new way of doing politics by inspiring hope, on the other (Dader 2015). Unlike 15M, this leadership is grounded on the idea of giving a single voice to many other voices and is capable of taking the demands from the street to inside the political system (Palao Errando 2015a). In this way, *Podemos* channelled the polyphony of 15M voices into a single voice through a media-based leadership, while at the same time maintaining a substantial part of the base of the *indignados*' political discourse. Following the European elections of 2014, and in the campaign leading up to the general elections of 2015 and June 2016, the role of such a prominent leader in the media has aroused tensions in the party's grassroots. Calls for the redistribution of power and responsibilities in the party's internal organisation were heard.

One key instance of the use of this leadership tactic in the 2014 European election campaign was the last-minute decision to replace the party logo on the ballot paper with a sketch of Iglesias's face. This unprecedented move was taken by campaign coordinator Iñigo Errejón, who later defined his decision as 'decisive' and defended it as 'a strategic use of central leadership in [*Podemos*'s] political operation' (Errejón 2014). In the two months prior to the European election, only 6 per cent of Spanish citizens were aware of *Podemos*'s existence, whereas 50 per cent were familiar with Iglesias (López García 2015). Iglesias, the political leader, was turned into an electoral brand.

Underlying this decision were the party founders' pragmatic attitudes and their mediatisation of politics as a strategy to succeed in the polls. Errejón concludes that Pablo Iglesias's media-based leadership was a *sine qua non* condition and precipitated a process of building hope and participation in the 2014 European elections (Errejón 2014).

In terms of communication, *Podemos* chose to strengthen the media logic by using simple emotional messages, appropriate for television. The brand image was promoted above and beyond the political or ideological programme, and pushing the candidate's image was in line with political marketing principles. Using Pablo Iglesias's face on the ballot paper was another stage in this process.

Social media as Podemos's natural habitat

The use of social media in the 2004 European election campaign was another key factor in *Podemos*'s rapid rise. Social media was the natural space for this new party, which included 15M participants in its team, particularly those from *Juventud sin Futuro* ('Youth with no Future'). This group experimented widely with social media for activism by using hashtags, circulating information, organising events and the like. Eduardo Fernández Rubiño, head of social media for *Podemos*, has highlighted the importance of 15M as a testing ground in using social media for political purposes, and he considers these platforms to be ideal environments for political intervention (Fernández Rubiño 2015).

Podemos's growth in the social media during the 2014 campaign considerably outstripped that of the traditional parties (Gómez & Viejo 2014). In its first three months, *Podemos* built up a Twitter following similar to that of the traditional parties. On the day of the elections, *Podemos* had 139,473 followers on Twitter, as compared with the

PSOE's 139,510 and 140,255 following the PP.[19] Differences on Facebook were even greater, with *Podemos* showing the highest growth of all the Spanish political parties in the 3 months up to polling day, when *Podemos* had 209,236 Facebook followers, as compared with the PP's 64,084 and the PSOE's 60,956.[20]

According to Fernández Rubiño, this growth is due to the fact that the traditional parties have never really stopped to think about the idiosyncrasies of the social media. Digital media is regarded as a broadcasting mechanism for issues already decided elsewhere, and the distinctive features of the digital media are not taken into account (Fernández Rubiño 2015). The traditional conception of the main parties, following the mainstream media logic and the theory of the normalisation of political communication in the digital environment (Margolis & Resnick 2000), is reflected in the use of social media. Candidates heading the PP and PSOE lists in the 2014 European elections, Arias Cañete and Elena Valenciano, respectively, are examples. Arias Cañete created his profile in April 2014, just before the campaign began, and tweeted on only 92 occasions with typical campaign photographs, attacks on the opposition and impersonal, non-interactive messages. Elena Valenciano used Twitter slightly more during the campaign, although her account had been closed for months. She tweeted an average of nine times a day with standard electoral campaign comments and photographs of her activities. After the elections her account registered no activity for days. This use of social networks by these two political leaders follows the parameters of 'controlled interactivity', which makes pretence of digital participation (Stromer-Galley 2014).

In contrast, Pablo Iglesias's Twitter account had been active since June 2010 and attracted a large number of followers (150,000 at the end of the European elections and 1,838,545 in August 2016). *Podemos*'s growth in the use of social media was such that it became an uninterrupted trending topic during the last week of the 2014 European election campaign, including polling day itself, with the use of various hashtags. The reason for this, according to Fernández Rubiño, is that the social networks are central to *Podemos*'s political process; the contents published on them attract attention precisely because of the spontaneity these platforms offer the party (Fernández Rubiño 2015).

Podemos tailored its European election campaign to each social media platform. On Facebook it used emotional content; Twitter provided a space to share information quickly and to interact with other networks and groups. It also encouraged an open structure of fan pages and regional accounts through the *círculos*, consolidating a wide network with a strong central hub and an extensive list of accounts and profiles. Fernández Rubiño (2015) notes that Twitter was particularly important. It was a platform where users could find information about what was happening and could intervene to defend their own positions, register their complaints and call others to account.

The base of the party's territorial organisation, the *círculos*, spread simply and rapidly through the social networks. In turn, these *círculos* became key drivers in the 2014 election campaign. Their undefined function, together with the need to meet the challenge of presenting candidates in elections in the first three months of the party's existence, turned the *círculos* into mouthpieces for *Podemos*'s message across the whole of Spain. The mushrooming of 200 *círculos* during the European election campaign, involving thousands of activists and supporters, was 'an essential element driving the territories and the campaign' (Toret 2015, p. 130). By October 2014, the number of *círculos* had risen to 800, with 165,000 people registered. The party's subsequent evolution has prompted a crisis in the role of these organisational units; they are no longer spontaneous and chaotic, but strictly controlled by central party managers. The institutionalisation of the party has weakened the *círculos* and curtailed their once ample sovereignty and political autonomy. The inefficiency of their assembly structure, the mono-polisation of activities by small groups of activists and the centralisa-tion of party activities in the hands of party leaders have weakened their importance (Casero-Ripollés, Feenstra & Tormey 2016).

Conclusions: democratic innovations and contributions from the field of political communication

Two communication models emerged from 15M in Spain: one was linked to online political activism developed in the first stage of the movement; and the second was applied by *Podemos*. Both introduce significant innovations in the field of political communication, which have important implications for democracy. Both came out of social movements, both are led by actors on the margins of the political system, and both have had a significant impact in the way they have influenced news coverage in the mainstream media. Issues, approaches and discourses have been introduced into Spanish public debate.

The two models recognise that communication is central to political action, and communication lies at the heart of their activity. Unlike traditional political parties that tag communication onto the end of the political process, both *Podemos* and the 15M political activists start their process with communication. It is given a leading political and strategic role, which goes beyond the standard instrumental conception of communication. As a result, it is used to inform the public about political proposals and decisions and to win their support at election time. Communication retains these functions but goes beyond them. Communication forms the base of a political project, acts as a vehicle in the endeavour to establish the discursive meaning of political problems, frames reality, creates political identities and, in the final instance, generates a hegemonic vision that brings legitimacy and citizen support. This conception of communication and discourse as essential ingredients of the political dynamic is clearly present in *Podemos*'s underlying principles (which are decisive in informing its strategy at every level) and also, although less noticeably, in the political activism of 15M.

The central role of communication has prompted significant changes in the way these movements relate to the mainstream media. Although social movements have traditionally been hostile to the media, the leaders of *Podemos* and the 15M activists accept that the mainstream media hold a central position in political communication, in accordance with the mediatisation theory. They recognise that they must build relationships with mainstream media. Each model has a different formula, one based on overturning and the other on reshaping the mediatisation of politics. Both come to the same conclusion: the mainstream media continue to be the gatekeepers controlling the social visibility of political actors and their messages, setting the agenda and articulating public debate in democratic societies such as Spain. Although there is some mistrust of the mainstream media, this does not lead to abstention or a refusal to relate to them. Indeed, the search for and implementation of mechanisms to influence media coverage is one of the bases of their communication strategy.

The two communication models emerging from 15M are also innovative, a characteristic that suggests significant democratic potential. Overturning the media logic by using social media to generate a bottom-up, or reverse, agenda through sophisticated digital campaigns reflects how relationships among political communication actors are being reconfigured. This overturning is possible because it engages citizens, through activism, as active subjects in the public debate. On social media and digital spaces, citizens can find formulas where they can influence the media and political actors, not always without difficulty, and include their own issues and frames on the public agenda. Citizens, therefore, abandon the role of passive observers assigned to them by the mainstream media, especially television, in which their engagement in the interactions and discussions of others was limited, if not totally absent. Although the mainstream media are still the central players on the political communication stage, as the main source of information and the arena for the social representation of politics, they are now having to open up their news agendas and programmes to new civil society actors. The communication model of activism created by 15M has shown this change can be made, and if it is generalised, expanded and consolidated, it could have significant implications for democracy.

For its part, *Podemos*'s communication strategy makes an innovative contribution by renovating and extending the theory of the mediatisation of politics. The party's model, linked to its 15M origins, embodies the hybridisation of current political communication by combining old and new logics and taking the best aspects of each one. It is this strategy that defines it as a transmedia party.

Podemos redefines our understanding of the mediatisation of politics by opening up a model of two-way cooperation outside of the predominant media-centric vision (Casero-Ripollés, Feenstra & Tormey 2016). The *Podemos* case shows that mediatisation can also occur in the opposite direction, from politics to the media, with the former influencing the latter. Non-media factors can also activate and drive this process. The case of *Podemos* illustrates this in various ways: by using social media to generate citizen involvement, fashioning Iglesias's leadership, using knowledge about how television works to 'hack' into it and simplifying the political message to engage with citizens' emotions. In its 2014 European election campaign, *Podemos* showed that adapting to the rules and criteria of the mainstream media is not the only response. Other actions and communication strategies are possible, without abandoning the mediatisation of politics theory.

This two-way mediatisation, together with the combination and interrelation between mainstream and digital media, allowed *Podemos* to 'leap into' traditional media, the main mechanism of political socialisation today. From the centre of Spanish political debate, they gained access to and took part in constructing the political agenda. It is here that the democratic potential of this strategy lies, since it offers an incipient political subject, located on the margins of institutional politics, the chance to take up a central position and leading role in the political dynamic.

In both *Podemos*'s and the 15M activists' communication models, technology is incorporated as a determinant of political communication. Both are based on orchestrating a multi-layered strategy (Toret 2015) that combines three spheres with differing strengths: the street (or citizen political mobilisation), the digital environment (led by the social media) and the mainstream media (mainly television, but also the newspapers). While the 15M activists focused on the digital environment and later turned to the other two spheres, *Podemos* centred its attention on the mainstream media, particularly television. While the 15M activists devised an unprecedented model based on overturn, *Podemos* renewed the theory of mediatisation. In practice, this incorporated the politics-to-media channel and turned a relatively closed system with a limited number of news sources into an open, multi-platform scenario teeming with information (Keane 2013; Chadwick 2013). *Podemos*'s communication model, therefore, corresponds to what may be called two-way mediatisation, bringing this theory up to date and helping to extend it, as several scholars have already called for (Mattoni & Treré 2014).

Both models make significant innovations in political communication, through the original ways of doing things or by reshaping the established dynamics. Similarly, the models have considerable democratic potential: They contribute to reshaping relationships among political communication actors, enabling citizens to take on an influential role and opening up opportunities to political actors on the margins of the institutional political system (e.g. activists, social movements and new parties) to participate in political debate. They provide a channel that makes inclusive opportunity possible (Blumler & Coleman 2015) and, through communication, allows social groups with alternative political frames to be recognised and heard. It is here that the Spanish political laboratory also makes significant contributions to political communication for reshaping democracy.

Notes

1 http://agorasolradio.blogspot.com.
2 www.tomalatele.tv/web/.
3 http://madrid15m.org.
4 http://diagonalperiodico.net.
5 https://directa.cat.
6 http://periodismohumano.com.
7 http://madrilonia.org.
8 See for example (in Spanish): https://docs.google.com/document/d/19wuz7w KyykbKYfimFgOddGbGGW2degtGmeHo87YwWUI/view or http://ma llorca.democraciarealya.es/2013/04/03/manual-de-iniciacion-a-las-campana s-activistas-en-twitter/.
9 The founders of *Podemos* included Pablo Iglesias, Iñigo Errejón, Juan Carlos Monedero, Carolina Bescansa and Luis Alegre. For information on other key actors, see (in Spanish): http://politica.elpais.com/politica/2014/ 11/15/actualidad/1416083204_351563.html.
10 Lecture '*Los límites de la manipulación: otra información es posible*' in the 2012 summer school '*Poder, Ideología y medios de comunicación*',

Academia de Pensamiento Crítico. Available (in Spanish) at: www.youtube.com/watch?v=nfK2Bl4NjGM (Minutes: 13:22–1s3:45).

11 Available at: https://www.youtube.com/watch?v=o3me4hDrbzU.
12 Programme available at: www.youtube.com/watch?v=5dKkeGybvFw.
13 See the following excepts as examples: www.youtube.com/watch?v=MwkJMOo Ai-M, www.youtube.com/watch?v=T9fuT3eCSvQ, www.youtube.com/watch? v=zHpUPHzKuLc and www.youtube.com/watch?v=4AZ6l_erQeo&list= PL3Z1dC0Z6FGB-YHMccJON58Du4rpyoxKg.
14 www.youtube.com/watch?v=s9S1oktKbBs.
15 Extract from Pablo Iglesias' contribution to the talk 'What is a real democracy?' held at the Sala Mirador on 5 February 2014: https://www.youtube.com/watch?v=Yizw-RySZnI (Minutes: 2:07–2:11).
16 Campaign video (in Spanish) available at: https://www.youtube.com/watch?v=unFxEn2gcTs.
17 "Democracy: What is a real democracy?" Lecture (in Spanish) with Alberto Garzón and Pablo Iglesias, 6 February 2014. Available at: www.youtube.com/watch?v=eDYDSQlF0go (Minutes: 1:03.28–1:05.12).
18 Interview (in Spanish) with Juan Carlos Monedero. Attac TV. 27 September 2015. Available at: www.attac.tv/2013/09/18602 (Minutes: 18:26–17:22)
19 As of 29 August 2016, these differences in Twitter followers continue to rise: *Podemos*, 1,130,670; *Partido Popular* (PP), 572,600; and *Partido Socialista Obrero Español* (PSOE), 459,275.
20 Data is available at: http://smetrica.com/ As of 29 August 2016, differences in Facebook 'likes' are even greater: *Podemos*, 1,092,428; *Partido Popular* (PP), 160,037; and *Partido Socialista Obrero Español* (PSOE), 135,324.

Conclusions: the Spanish political laboratory in action

The debate summarised in what follows leaves no doubt about the extraordinary period of political agitation witnessed in Spain since the events of 15 May 2011. Demonstrations were triggered in more than 55 cities across the country involving millions of Spanish citizens. Citizen participation and expression have since flourished in multiple forms. From the start, 15M activists and supporters were united in their rejection of corruption, their anger and indignation at the inability of the political elites to provide honest leadership in times of crisis, and the feeling that Spanish democracy had been hijacked and degraded.

As it became increasingly clear that the political elites neither could, nor wanted to, take this citizen uprising seriously, the process of rethinking leadership, debate and experimentation began to permeate Spanish society. This change was expressed in spontaneous *acampadas*, which sought some kind of semi-permanent institutionalisation in the form of assemblies. Under the slogan of 'real democracy', and to highlight the gap between promise and reality in the Spanish democratic system, citizens began to create parallel institutions and processes. They wanted to shame politicians into acknowledging their own lack of democratic legitimacy and the shortcomings of the existing parliamentary and electoral processes. In this context, the marked anti-representative nature of this succession of events should be kept in mind. The *acampadas* and assemblies eroded the authority of the idea of parliamentary representation as *the* base for democratic life. It was as though Jacques Rancière's vision of democracy, as an external dynamic kicking against top-down 'politics of the police', had come to life and been set in motion by the citizens themselves (Rancière 2006a, 2006b).

We now know that the public's energies waned and citizen protests began to fall off. Things went back to 'normal' – at least that is what appeared to happen. The spell of parliamentary representation, however, had clearly been broken, as reflected in one of the banners hung in Madrid's Puerta del Sol de Madrid: 'This isn't a crisis; what it means is I don't love you anymore'. Faith in the democratic credentials of the Spanish political system had crumbled. Citizens asked what might be the key political question: in practice, how can the search for an improved democracy be sustained, and what might that mean?

All types of democratic experimentation outside the realms of conventional parliamentary politics have taken place since 2011, including numerous variations on direct action initiatives taken forward notably by the PAH and the *iai@flautas*. Other experiments include the formation of new groups, autonomous self-managing initiatives, and networks to protect and support citizens in precarious economic situations. A wide range of monitoring mechanisms have appeared and are described throughout this book, including platforms to combat corruption, cronyism, clientelism and the long list of failures perpetrated by the Spanish economic and political elites. New strategies and repertoires of digital action have also been devised to influence the media agenda and encourage subversion of the media logic through innovative models of political communication. Finally, the new political parties also form part of the same lively, although surprising, dynamic. As we have noted throughout this book, part of the energy driving the 15M movement was related to the feeling that parliamentary representation was not fulfilling its role as a solid foundation on which to organise democratic life. It was precisely the gap between *representatives* and *represented* that was considered to be an insuperable problem. The domination of Spanish politics over the last 40 years by two major political parties, PP and PSOE, was viewed by many citizens as the cause of the corrupt, moribund state of democratic life. For that reason, one of the most interesting outcomes of this democratic experimentation is the proliferation of new parties. The activists' realisation that substantial political changes would have to go hand in hand with a clear commitment to elections, parliaments and institutions is one of the main features of the current circumstances. *Podemos's* results in the European elections of May 2014 galvanised commitment in this direction. The realisation that there is an electorate for this message of renewal has led to fresh interest in developing and creating political parties that embrace 'the street', on one hand, and 'parliament', on the other. In hundreds of towns and cities across Spain, political agendas have prioritised reflection on such issues as the significance of elections, strategic alliances, the strengths and weaknesses of parliaments, what is meant by good leadership and the future of political parties.

What is clear is that events in Spain are transforming the basic coordinates of traditional democratic life. In Europe and elsewhere, since the end of the 18th century when the basic principles of representative democracy were forged (Keane 2009), we have routinely accepted the distinction between the elites who represent and the rest who are represented. We have become inured to a politics that happens in the upper echelons, in one specific institutional space – parliament – carried out by specific actors – political parties and politicians – who are accountable for their actions from time to time in the polls. We conform to a standard set of political actions that offers us two ways to participate: 1) activism in and through political party membership; and 2) activism through 'participation' in the form of, for example, voting every so many years, and pressure, petitions and protests against parliament and in the streets.

As this book shows, these coordinates are becoming increasingly problematic and difficult to maintain as the logic of representative democracy is being reassessed. Activists who have to date fought their battles in the streets are not only setting up political parties but also, as seen in local council and regional elections in 2015, gaining access to positions of power. Ada Colau can no longer be regarded as a 'street activist'. Following her election as Barcelona's mayor, she is now at the forefront of action *within* the political process. She largely came to fame for drawing attention to the shortcomings of the established political elite and of the very democratic process itself. Given that this is such a new phenomenon, what does it portend? Where are these events taking us?

As we have noted throughout this book, it is not clear where these events will lead us. Two possible connected and overlapping trajectories of where the spirit and essence of democratic politics might take us come to mind. One succinct and useful way of describing the first of these two trajectories is what we refer to in this book as *monitory democracy* (Keane 2009, 2013). The other possibility is associated with an alternative form of political democracy we term *post-representative democracy* (Tormey 2015a, 2015b). A brief reflection on each of these may help stimulate debate on possible future scenarios of politics in Spain.

Monitory democracy

The theory of monitory democracy highlights how our generation's democratic politics is trapped in a long-term historic change. This trend diverts citizens' attention away from elections, parliaments and politicians to focus on examining and controlling the arbitrary exercise of power wherever it takes place, whether at national government level, in the markets, in civil society or in cross-border settings. According to this argument, in the era of monitory democracy citizen political activity is not restricted to elections, parties and parliaments – that is, formal parliamentary politics in its strictest sense. New forms of non-party representative politics, involving those not elected in the polls, flourish in opposition to the traditional political parties. Seen from this perspective, the innovations appearing in the Spanish political labora-tory are of fundamental political importance; citizens' efforts to draw attention to institutionalised corruption, secrecy, violence and social injustice are essential because they demonstrate the *limits* of political parties and parliaments. This means that rather than witnessing the end of representative politics, events in Spain suggest that we are now facing a twofold democratic challenge: to revitalise the party political forms as trustworthy representatives of citizens' desires and needs; and the difficult and potentially complementary struggle to extend the principles of citizen participation and representation to all spheres of power where the arbitrary exercise of power prevails,

Monitory democracy warns against blind belief in the 'top-down' rule. In defence of democratising power, it opposes the arrogance and abuse of power, and for this reason it is better understood as a struggle to scrutinise, stop and inform about the arbitrary exercise of political and socio-economic power, even in cross-border environments. It extends the notion that citizens are no longer – assuming that they once were – mere passive uninformed spectators of the political process that goes by outside their everyday experience. Monitory democracy theory pays particular attention to the role that digital technologies, communicative abundance and journalism, both traditional and alter-native, play in generating opportunities for citizens and their repre-sentatives to publicly question and reject unaccountable power (Keane 2013). WikiLeaks is among the most forceful contemporary examples of this fledgling politics, enabled by communicative abundance. Whereas previously it would have been extremely difficult and danger-ous to publish confidential communications about the activities of states and their diverse diplomatic and military adventures, now this information can be directly placed at the public's disposal, with all the political consequences this entails.

In this new era, monitory democracy has given new 'weapons to the weak', in some way turning relations of power upside down. Citizens and their representatives have been given a considerable advantage against the secretive and petulant elites that could previously do what they wanted in splendid isolation, out of public sight and mind. As a result, power now rarely intervenes from inaccessible places or dark corners. It is subject to greater scrutiny and questioning and to more solid efforts to stop and control its arbitrariness and harmful effects. Citizens have now been empowered to see themselves as actors in their own right and with a moral responsibility to challenge power. This new attitude questions and undermines the idea of politics and politicians being in some way 'special', either in terms of vocation or substantial political content (Weber 1978). Citizens are gradually gaining enough strength to exercise their own influence, to demonstrate in practice the power of 'those without power' and to ensure that their interests have a voice and are protected and satisfied.

Some observers have argued that, in practice, monitory democracy does not question the legitimacy of democratic representation. These stances, however, are based on the misinterpretation of the innovations consolidated in the era of monitory democracy. All politics certainly involves presenting claims on behalf of others (Saward 2010, 2011); yet this new ecology of political representation is no longer limited to elections, parties and parliaments – that is, formal parliamentary politics. Direct citizen involvement frequently erupts in opposition to the traditional political parties, backed by non-party or non-elected representative politics, but representing civil society groups. This is a key reason why in many places, including Spain, political parties are finding themselves in trouble. Increasingly, they have to compete in areas of power with other citizen-backed organisations that claim to represent their electorate. From the monitory democracy viewpoint, we are not witnessing the end of representative politics but living through an era in which the ecology of representation is changing, becoming more complex and more dispersed. It follows that the main political struggle is no longer – or at least not predominantly – the battle for 'one person, one vote', as it was from the 18th century until around 1945. In the era of monitory democracy, the predominant struggle is to establish the principle of 'one person, many votes, many representatives', as opposed to the perilous concentrations of arbitrary power, wherever they might be.

There is strong evidence of monitory democracy in Spain, seen in the constant questioning and accusation of the elites by many different citizen initiatives. This has had the effect of transforming the public's perception of politicians, parties and state institutions as a whole. The aura previously surrounding the political class is clearly being replaced by public disdain and ridiculing of parliamentary politics every time a new scandal breaks on the internet, in the mainstream media or the expanding alternative media. The Spanish elites see their situation as compromised; this trend is largely in line with the thesis of monitory democracy which tells us we should get used to seeing worried expressions on the faces of our elites. Previously self-confident in their ability to obtain favourable results for themselves and their clients, they are now being cornered in the spotlight of public scrutiny. The proliferation of new political parties can also be interpreted under the lens of monitory democracy. Many of the incipient parties and platforms, such as *Podemos, Ahora Madrid* and *Barcelona en Común*, prioritise greater decision-making transparency, restriction and public control over the banking and credit industry, and control of the activities of politicians and the traditional political parties. In other words, these 'monitoring parties' are themselves expressions of the same concepts that are driving other types of monitoring mechanisms, such as NGOs or platforms against social and political injustice. These new parties embody monitory democracy in action. To a certain extent they are citizen expressions of distrust and scepticism over the activities of political elites that do not justify their actions to the public. The big difference is that the new monitoring parties are competing for governmental power against the established political elite; as a result, *they themselves* have to address the question of how to respond to the same forces, expectations and pressures associated with monitory democracy. This has put pressure on these new parties to develop codes of conduct, ethics statutes and practices to put their supporters' and voters' minds at rest. They seem to have learned the lesson that the traditional parties have not taken on board: from now on, exercise of power must be visible, transparent and subject to public limitation and control.

Post-representation

Is there anything in these contemporary developments that takes us beyond the problematic that is set out in the frame of monitory democracy? At the core of 15M and its political legacy lies the way it questions and re-examines the very foundation of electoral representation as the base of democratic development. The legacy of this thought lies in a series of motifs; for example, in the form of the assembly which remains an important point of reference, or central idea, when considering how to engage citizens in politics. In its early days, *Podemos* used the *círculos* structure; other new political groups, especially those connected to municipal council movements, still maintain close links with their grassroots supporters through assemblies. The new digital tools are also a fascinating way of directly engaging citizens in discussions and decision making. Throughout the book, we have described initiatives designed to stimulate direct democracy by extending or, in some cases, replacing the representative function with direct online decision-making mechanisms. More generally, the rhetoric of new political parties such as *Podemos* firmly continues to address *la casta* and the idea of the political class as a group whose interests do not include citizens and civil society. This implies that citizens themselves must narrow the distance between representatives and the represented, rather than glorifying this distance as a new version of representative democracy.

From the second viewpoint, parliamentary-representative democracy is not only a faded imitation of the democratic ideal, but is also a mechanism to prevent ordinary citizens from exercising greater control over their own lives. Of course, the alternative is easier to describe than put into practice. Despite all the optimism about the internet's potential for citizen participation, this view of post-representation politics is still more wishful thinking than a fully developed alternative to the forms of traditional representation.

The fact that there is an attitude of hostility towards parliaments and other forms of representation, however, casts a shadow over current events and initiatives, including the appearance of new political parties. As well as having to consider how they can be more transparent, these new parties must also modify some aspects of the political party as a vehicle for political representation, such as putting in place measures to prevent new elites from springing up within them. Several parties have already introduced mechanisms to rotate official positions, to effect revocation and to reduce salaries for elected positions. These and other measures may be understood as defence mechanisms – that is, ways of stopping power from taking hold and preventing figures and personalities in these new parties from becoming arrogant. This obviously has its limits. In the area of political leadership, for example, much of *Podemos*'s success is due to the easily identifiable figure of Pablo Iglesias; *Ahora Madrid* would not be where it is now without Manuela Carmena; and *Barcelona en Común*'s election campaign would not have had the same success without the formidable presence of Ada Colau. To what extent is political leadership emerging as a *performative* characteristic of the new politics, as opposed to a substantial element of their identity as political actors? How is it possible to avoid what seems to be an inherent oxymoron of the new politics – an anti-representative style of representative politics?

These are complicated questions that help to explain why the second course described here is what we refer to as 'post-representative'. The prefix *post-* denotes a paradox at the core of contemporary political life. In a media-saturated environment, where political actions are carried out on a scale involving millions of citizens, many of these citizens come to politics through the projection of personalities in the mainstream and digital media. After all, there is nothing *outside* the mass media in such an environment; and in consequence, neither is there anything outside politics as a *form* of representation. There will always be political leaders, charismatic personalities and visible figureheads who adopt and embody a particular stance on the major questions of the moment; they provide a focus for the ordinary person's attention. The mechanisms of representation are unavoidable and essential if we understand them as they were defended by the first guardians of representative democracy: acting on behalf of others, in their name, and subject to their consent. At the same time, we are witnessing the evolution or appearance of political figures whose foundations and *raison d'être* are to reject the legacy of the traditional political leader – the politician as representative. These are the 'post-representatives' – representatives who are simultaneously 'monitory and monitored', even though they have their roots in criticism of the very legacy of politics and politicians.

Looking to the future

The controversial ambivalence about parliamentary representation among millions of Spanish citizens is fully understandable. Our analysis suggests that simply going back to the mass political parties with their memberships of millions seems to be highly improbable. On this point the perspectives of monitory and post-representative democracy firmly coincide. As Robert Michels (1998 [1915]) stated in his landmark book *Political Parties*, in their heyday parties were powerful patronage machines, providing their fee-paying members and supporters with significant benefits in the form of jobs, training, financial support and access to state power and its resources. Today's parties tend to be ghostly and often corrupted shadows of their former selves, which poses the following questions. Given that political parties, in one way or another, continue to be indispensable mechanisms for accessing state resources, such as tax revenue, legislative power and police and military forces, what type of political party would be more likely to succeed in the polls and in winning citizens' support? Can a new post-representative politics be maintained when facing these challenges? Will the incipient political parties, with their lighter and more horizontal structures, drive the use of digital tools to empower their sympathisers and enable them to participate? Alternatively, will they use multimedia tactics and algorithms such as Google – good for appealing to the emotions and mobilising votes – within the framework of controlled interaction and closer to Michels's model of the traditional mass party?

These questions lead us to what may be the most interesting part of the Spanish democratic laboratory. The above-mentioned political figures are linked to forms of decision making and deliberation that have their origins in civil society groups. They are against the traditional forms of executive power with issues we are so used to reporting in Western parliamentary democracies: too many special interests, too many privileged players, smokescreens, revolving doors, shady alliances and money in brown envelopes.

But it is on this point that numerous observers have questioned just how this more direct political alternative can be put into practice. Can the gap between the represented and the representatives be reduced through social networks and new digital tools? And if so, where does that leave those who are unfamiliar with such technologies, the homeless, and people who have no access to online participatory digital media? Where does it leave those who, for whatever reason, are not attracted by this new 'click power'? Does it imply a desire to keep up the overwhelming impetus of the public forums and assemblies, the memory of which is still very much alive in the minds of many activists in the Spanish democratic laboratory? And if this is the case, is this not a formula for what has been termed 'the tyranny of structurelessness'[1] – that is, transferring the burden to ordinary citizens who have the time, energy and means to spend hours in public debates? Is it not simply a case of making a fetish of 'presence' over 'voice' regardless of how weak or mediated it is by other processes? Why should those with responsibilities for looking after their children or older relatives, or those who have to go to work, have to become hostages of those who are 'crazy about politics' and are perfectly happy to spend all their free time in group debates? Is there no argument to suggest that this practice looks less to the future than to the past, based perhaps on the nostalgic desire for face-to-face, neighbourhood interactions, a slower, community-based way of life, and other tropes that go back to the assembly democracy of classical Greece? Bearing in mind the patterns and trends of contemporary society, the question arises of whether the danger of this nostalgic ambition is that it starts to move away from the reality of many citizens' lives. We have neither the time nor the means to play the role of what the direct models of democracy would like us to be, and so we have to move away from the ideal of the citizen of ancient Athens. Why? Unlike the ancient Greeks, we fortunately do not have slaves to do our dirty work. Perhaps because representation – that is, demands and actions carried out on other people's behalf, with their consent – is often a positive characteristic that cannot be eradicated from public life (Flinders 2012). This characteristic seems to be corroborated in Spain with the shift from the slogan 'They don't represent us' to that of 'We represent ourselves'.

Whatever happens to representative politics, the fact that we are now debating a range of democratic practices within the spectrum of institutional designs testifies to the central idea that we have tried to put across in this book: that we are observing an extraordinary desire to rethink the basic coordinates of democratic life in Spain. It is not easy to think of another modern political system where this sense of contingency runs so deep, and where the alternatives seem so real, as in Spain. Might the Spanish testing ground have a much greater, and potentially global importance? Is it a new, more radical phase of the spirit and essence of monitory democracy in every area of institutionalised power? Or might the Spanish revolt against parliamentary representation indicate the birth of a new type of post-representative politics, a 'politics of resonance' (Tormey 2015a) with citizens, not politicians, at its heart? Nobody yet knows the answers to these major political questions of our times, and that is why the ongoing experiments in the Spanish laboratory are so fascinating and stimulating, and of global importance.

Note

1 See www.jofreeman.com/joreen/tyranny.htm.

References

Abensour, M. (2011) *Democracy against the State: Marx and the Machiavellian Moment*. Cambridge: Polity Press.

Allan, S., & Thorsen, E. (2009) *Citizen Journalism: Global Perspectives*. New York: Peter Lang.

Alonso, S. (2014) "Votas Pero no Eliges: La Democracia y la Crisis de la Deuda Soberana en la Eurozona", *Recerca: Revista de Pensament i Anàlisi*, 15: 21–53.

Alonso-Muñoz, L., & Casero-Ripollés, A. (2016) "La Influencia del Discurso sobre Cambio Social en la Agenda de los Medios: El Caso de la Plataforma de Afectados por la Hipoteca", *Obets*, 11(1): 25–51.

Altheide, D. L., & Snow, R. P. (1979) *Media Logic*. Beverly Hills, CA: Sage.

Anduiza, E., Cristancho, C., & Sabucedo, J. M. (2014) "Mobilization through Online Social Networks: The Political Protest of the Indignados in Spain", *Communication and Society*, 17(6): 750–764.

Atton, C. (2002) *Alternative Media*. London: Sage.

Badiou, A. (1989) *Manifiesto por la Filosofía*. Madrid: Cátedra.

Baiocchi, G., & Ganuza, E. (2016) *Popular democracy: The paradox of participation*. Standford, CA: Stanford University Press.

Bakardjieva, M. (2012) "Reconfiguring the Mediapolis: New Media and Civic Agency", *New Media and Society*, 14(1): 63–79.

Barranquero Carretero, A., & Meda González, M. (2015) "Los Medios Comunitarios y Alternativos en el Ciclo de Protestas Ciudadanas desde el 15M", *Athenea Digital: Revista de Pensamiento e Investigación Social*, 15: 139–170.

Bennett, W. L., & Segerberg, A. (2012) "The Logic of Connective Action: Digital Media and the Personalization of Contentious Politics", *Information, Communication and Society*, 15(5): 739–768.

Bennett, W. L., & Segerberg, A. (2013) *The Logic of Connective Action: Digital Media and the Personalization of Contentious Politics*. New York: Cambridge University Press.

Benski, T., Langman, L., Perugorría, I., & Tejerina, B. (2013) "From the Streets and Squares to Social Movement Studies: What have we learned?", *Current Sociology*, 61(4): 541–561.

Bjornlund, E. C. (2004) *Beyond Free and Fair: Monitoring Elections and Building Democracy*. Baltimore, MD: Johns Hopkins University Press.

Blumler, J. G., & Coleman, S. (2015) "Democracy and the Media – Revisited", *Javnost – The Public*, 22(2): 111–128.

Cabannes, Y. (2004) "Participatory Budgeting: A Significant Contribution to Participatory Democracy", *Environment and Urbanization*, 16(1): 27–46.

Calvo, P. (2015) "Whistleblowing ante la Miseria Moral de Instituciones y Organizaciones". In Avilés Hernández, M., & Meseguer Sánchez, J. V. (eds) *Empresas, Derechos Humanos y RSC*. Pamplona: Aranzadi, 135–153.

Cammaerts, B. (2012) "Protest Logics and the Mediation Opportunity Structure", *European Journal of Communication*, 27(2): 117–134.

Candón Mena, J. I. (2013) *Toma la Calle, Toma las Redes: El Movimiento #15M en Internet*. Sevilla: Atrapasueños.

Casas, A., Davesa, F., & Congosto, M. (2016) "La Cobertura Mediática de una Acción «conectiva»: La Interacción entre el Movimiento 15-M y los Medios de Comunicación", *Reis*, 155: 73–96.

Casero-Ripollés, A. (2008) "Modelos de Relación entre Periodistas y Políticos: La Perspectiva de la Negociación Constante", *Estudios Sobre el Mensaje Periodístico*, 14: 111–128.

Casero-Ripollés, A. (2010) "¿El Despertar del Público?: Comunicación Política, Ciudadanía y Web 2.0". In Martin Vicente, M., & Rothberg, D. (eds) *Meios de Comunicaçao e Cidadania*. São Paulo, Brazil: Cultura Acadêmica, 107–122.

Casero-Ripollés, A., & Feenstra, R. A. (2012) "The 15-M Movement and the New Media: A Case Study of How New Themes Were Introduced into Spanish Political Discourse", *Media International Australia*, 144(1): 68–76.

Casero-Ripollés, A., Feenstra, R. A., & Tormey, S. (2016) "Old and New Media Logics in an Electoral Campaign: The Case of Podemos and the Two-Way Street Mediatization of Politics", *International Journal of Press/Politics*, 21(3): 378–397.

Castañeda, E. (2012) "The Indignados of Spain: A Precedent to Occupy Wall Street", *Social Movement Studies*, 11(3–4): 309–319.

Castells, M. (2009) *Communication Power*. Oxford: Oxford University Press.

Castells, M. (2012) *Networks of Outrage and Hope: Social Movements in the Internet Age*. Malden, MA: Polity Press.

Chadwick, A. (2007) "Digital Network Repertoires and Organizational Hybridity", *Political Communication*, 24(3): 283–301.

Chadwick, A. (2013) *The Hybrid Media: Politics and Power*. Oxford: Oxford University Press.

Charnock, G., Purcell, T., & Ribera-Fumaz, R. (2011) "¡Indígnate!: The 2011 Popular Protest and the Limits to Democracy in Spain", *Capital and Class*, 36(1): 3–11.

Chester, J. (2007) *Digital Destiny: New Media and the Future of Democracy.* New York: The New Press.

Cortina, A. (1993) *Ética Aplicada y Democracia Radical.* Madrid: Tecnos.

Crouch, C. (2004) *Post-Democracy.* Cambridge: Polity Press.

Dader, J. L. (2015) "Fascinados por 'Podemos': Un Fenómeno Natural de la 'Democracia Sentimental'", *H-ermes: Journal of Communication*, 4: 13–45.

Dalton, R. J. (2002) *Citizen Politics: Public Opinion and Political Parties in Advanced Industrial Democracies.* London: Chatham House.

Dalton, R. J. (2004) *Democratic Challenges, Democratic Choices: The Erosion of Political Support in Advanced Industrial Democracies.* Oxford: Oxford University Press.

Davis, A. (2010) *Political Communication and Social Theory.* London: Taylor & Francis.

Day, R. (2004) "From Hegemony to Affinity: The Political Logic of the Newest Social Movements", *Cultural Studies*, 18(5): 716–748.

Deacon, D., & Stanyer, J. (2014) "Mediatization: Key Concept or Conceptual Bandwagon?", *Media, Culture & Society*, 36(7): 1032–1044.

Dean, J. (2009) *Democracy and Other Neoliberal Fantasies: Communicative Capitalism and Left Politics.* Durham, NC: Duke University Press.

Della Porta, D. (2011) "Communication in Movement: Social Movements as Agents of Participatory Democracy", *Information, Communication and Society*, 14(6): 800–819.

Della Porta, D. (2013) *Can Democracy Be Saved? Participation, Deliberation and Social Movements.* Cambridge: Polity Press.

Diani, M., & McAdam, D. (2003) *Social Movements and Networks: Relational Approaches to Collective Action.* Oxford: Oxford University Press.

Díaz, S., & Lozano, J. (eds) (2013) *Vigilados. Wikileaks o las Nuevas Formas de la Información.* Madrid: Biblioteca Nueva.

Downing, J. (2001) *Radical Media: Rebellious Communication and Social Movements.* London: Sage.

Earl, J., & Kimport, K. (2011) *Digitally Enabled Social Change: Activism in the Internet Age.* Cambridge, MA: MIT Press.

Errejón, I. (2011) "El 15-M como Discurso Contrahegemónico", *Encrucijadas*, 2: 120–145.

Errejón, I. (2014) "¿Qué es 'Podemos'?" *Le Monde Diplomatique*, 225, July. Retrieved from: www.monde-diplomatique.es/?url=articulo/00008564128721 68186811102294251000/?articulo=8c640f81-5ccc-4723-911e-71e45da1deca.

Esser, F., & Matthes, J. (2013) "Mediatization Effects on Political News, Political Actors, Political Decisions, and Political Audiences". In Kriesi, H., Bochsler, D., Matthes, J., Lavenex, S., Bühlmann, M., & Esser, F. (eds) *Democracy in the Age of Globalization and Mediatization.* Basingstoke: Palgrave Macmillan, 177–201.

Feenstra, R. A. (2012) *Democracia Monitoriza en la Era de la Nueva Galaxia Mediática.* Barcelona: Icaria.

Feenstra, R. A. (2015) "Activist and citizen political repertoire in Spain: A reflection based on civil society theorand different logics of political participation", *Journal of Civil Society*, 11(3): 242–258.

Feenstra, R. A., & Casero-Ripollés, A. (2014) "Democracy in the Digital Communication Environment: A Typology Proposal of Political Monitoring Processes", *International Journal of Communication*, 8: 2448–2468.

Feenstra, R. A., & Keane, J. (2014) "Politics in Spain: A Case of Monitory Democracy", *VOLUNTAS: International Journal of Voluntary and Nonprofit Organizations*, 25(5): 1262–1280.

Feenstra, R. A., Tormey, S., Casero-Ripollés, A., & Keane, J. (2016) *La Configuración de la Democracia: El Laboratorio Político Español*. Granada: Comares.

Fernández Rubiño, E. (2015) "Nuevas Formas de Cultura Política: Podemos, un Giro Anómalo de las Redes Sociales", *Teknokultura*, 12(1): 77–91.

Fernandez-Planells, A., Figueras-Maz, M., & Freixa, C. (2014) "Communication among Young People in the #spanishrevolution: Uses of Online–Offline Tools to Obtain Information about the #acampadabcn", *New Media & Society*, 16(8): 1287–1308.

Flesher Fominaya, C. (2007) "Autonomous Movements and the Institutional Left: Two Approaches in Tension in Madrid's Anti-Globalization Network", *South European Society & Politics*, 12(3): 335–358.

Flesher Fominaya, C. (2014a). *Social Movements and Globalizations: How Protest, Occupations and Uprising are Changing the World*. New York: Palgrave.

Flesher Fominaya, C. (2014b). "'Spain is Different': Podemos and 15-M", published online by Open Democracy, 29 May 2014. Retrieved from: www.opendemocracy. net/can-europe-make-it/cristina-flesher-fominaya/%E2%80%9Cspain-is-different %E2%80%9D-podemos-and-15m (accessed 15 June 2015).

Flinders, M. (2012) *Defending Politics: Why Democracy Matters in the Twenty-First Century*. Oxford: Oxford University Press.

FnfEurope (2013) "The Spanish Slump – Political Crisis and the Need for Institutional Reform". Brussels: Author. Retrieved from: http://fnf-europe. org/2013/06/17/the-spanish-slump-political-crisis-and-the-need-for-institution al-reform/ (accessed 27 November 2013).

Fuchs, C. (2010) "Alternative Media as Critical Media", *European Journal of Social Theory*, 13(2): 173–192.

Fuchs, C. (2014a). *Social Media: A Critical Introduction*. London: Sage.

Fuchs, C. (2014b). *OccupyMedia! The Occupy Movement and Social Media in Crisis Capitalism*. Winchester: Zero Books.

Gamson, W. A., & Wolfsfeld, G. (1993) "Movements and Media as Interacting Systems", *The Annals of the American Academy of Political and Social Science*, 528(1): 114–125.

Garcelon, M. (2006) "The 'Indymedia' Experiment: The Internet as Movement Facilitator against Institutional Control", *Convergence*, 12(1): 55–82.

García-Abadillo, M. T., Cebrián, F. J., & Moreno, R. R. (2015) "La Incidencia en España de la Reestructuración Bancaria en la Emisión de Participaciones Preferentes", *Estudios Financieros. Revista de Contabilidad y Tributación: Comentarios, Casos Prácticos* (388): 165–202.

García Marzá, D. (1998) "Desobediencia Civil". In Cortina, A. (ed.) *10 Palabras Clave en Filosofía Política*. Salamanca: Verbo Divino, 97–125.

García Marzá, D. (2008) "Sociedad Civil: Una Concepción Radical", *Recerca. Revista de Pensament i Anàlisi*, 8: 27–46.

García-Marzá, D. (2013) "Democracia de Doble vía: El No-Lugar de la Empresa en la Sociedad Civil", *Revista del Clad. Reforma y Democracia*, 57: 67–92.

Gerbaudo, P. (2012) *Tweets and the Streets: Social Media and Contemporary Activism*. London: Pluto Press.

Gitlin, T. (1980) *The Whole World Is Watching: Mass Media in the Making and Unmaking of the New Left*. Berkeley, CA: University of California Press.

Gladwell, M. (2010) "Small Change: Why the Revolution Will not be Tweeted", *The New Yorker*, 4 October: 42–49. Retrieved from: www.newyorker.com/magazine/2010/10/04/small-change-malcolm-gladwell.

Gómez, L., & Viejo, M. (2014) "Las Redes de Arrastre de Podemos". *El País*, 28 May. Retrieved from: http://politica.elpais.com/politica/2014/05/28/actualidad/1401305050_166293.html.

Graeber, D. (2013) *The Democracy Project. A History. A Crisis. A Movement.* New York: Penguin.

Gripsrud, J. (2009) "Digitising the Public Sphere: Two Key Issues", *Javnost – The Public Journal*, 16(1): 5–16.

Gutierrez-Rubí, A. (2011) *La Política Vigilada. La Comunicación Política en la Era de Wikileaks*. Barcelona: Universitat Oberta de Catalunya.

Habermas, J. (1998). *Facticidad y Validez*. Madrid: Trotta.

Harlow, S. (2012) "Social Media and Social Movements: Facebook and an Online Guatemalan Justice Movement that Moved Offline", *New Media and Society*, 14(2): 225–243.

Harlow, S., & Harp, D. (2013) "Alternative Media in a Digital Era: Comparing News and Information Use among Activists in the United States and Latin America", *Communication and Society*, 26(4): 25–51.

Harlow, S., & Johnson, T. (2011) "Overthrowing the Protest Paradigm? How The New York Times, Global Voices and Twitter Covered the Egyptian Revolution", *International Journal of Communication*, 5(16): 1359–1374. Retrieved from: http://ijoc.org/index.php/ijoc/article/view/1239.

Haro Barba, C., & Sampedro, V. (2011) "Activismo Político en Red: Del Movimiento por la Vivienda Digna al 15M", *Teknokultura*, 8(2): 157–175.

Hartley, J. (2009) "Journalism and Popular Culture". In Wahl-Jorgensen, K., & Hanitzsch, T. (eds) *The Handbook of Journalism Studies*. London: Routledge, 310–324.

Hindman, M. (2009) *The Myth of Digital Democracy*. Princeton, NJ: Princeton University Press.

Holloway, J. (2002) *Change the World Without Taking Power: The Meaning of Revolution Today.* London: Pluto Press.

Howard, P. N. (2005) *New Media Campaigns and the Managed Citizen.* Cambridge: Cambridge University Press.

Howarth, D. (2005) "Applying Discourse Theory: The Method of Articulation". In Howarth, D., & Torfing, J. (eds) *Discourse Theory in European Politics: Identity, Policy and Governance.* London: Palgrave, 317–349.

Hughes, N. (2011) "Young People Took to the Streets and all of a Sudden all of the Political Parties Got Old: The 15M Movement in Spain", *Social Movement Studies*, 10(4): 407–413.

Jenkins, H. (2006) *Convergence Culture: Where Old and New Media Collide.* New York: NYU Press.

Jensen, K. B. (2013) "Definitive and Sensitizing Conceptualizations of Mediatization", *Communication Theory*, 23(3): 203–222.

Jurado Gilabert, F. (2013) "Democracia 4.0: Desrepresentación en el Voto Telemático de las Leyes", *Revista Internacional de Pensamiento Político*, 8: 119–138.

Juris, J. S. (2005) "Social Forums and their Margins: Networking Logics and the Cultural Politics of Autonomous Space Ephemera Theory and Politics in Organization Forum", *Ephemera*, 5(2): 253–272.

Juris, J. S. (2008) *Networking Futures: The Movements against Corporate Globalization.* Durham, NC: Duke University Press.

Keane, J. (2005) *Whatever Happened to Democracy?* London: Big Ideas IPPR.

Keane, J. (2009) *The Life and Death of Democracy.* London: Simon & Schuster.

Keane, J. (2013) *Democracy and Media Decadence.* Cambridge: Cambridge University Press.

Kickert, W., & Ysa, T. (2014) "New Development: How the Spanish Government Responded to the Global Economic, Banking and Fiscal Crisis", *Public Money & Management*, 34(6): 453–457.

Kim, S. T., & Lee, Y. H. (2007) "New Functions of Internet Mediated Agenda-Setting: Agenda-Rippling and Reversed Agenda-Setting", *Korea Journalism Review*, 1(2): 3–29.

Kovach, B., & Rosenstiel, T. (2007) *The Elements of Journalism: What Newspeople Should Know and the Public Should Expect.* New York: Three Rivers Press.

Laclau, E. (1990) *New Reflections on the Revolutions of Our Time.* London: Verso.

Laclau, E. (1996) *Emancipation(s).* London: Verso.

Laclau, E. (2005) *La Razón Populista.* Buenos Aires: Fondo de Cultura Económica.

Lago, M. (2016) *Cartografía de los Recortes: El Gasto Público en España entre 2009 y 2014.* Madrid: Cuadernos de Acción Sindical. Retrieved from: www.pensamientocritico.org/comobr0516.pdf (accessed 4 September 2016).

Lathrop, D., & Ruma, L. (2010) *Open Government: Collaboration, Transparency, and Participation in Practice.* Sebastopol, CA: O'Reilly Media.

Lawson, K. (ed.) (2010) *Political Parties and Democracy.* Santa Barbara, CA: Praeger.

Lees-Marshment, J. S. (2011) *The Political Marketing Game*. Basingstoke: Palgrave Macmillan.

Lévy, P. (2001) *Cyberculture*. Minneapolis, MN: University of Minnesota Press.

Lievrouw, L. (2011) *Alternative and Activist New Media*. Cambridge: Polity Press.

Lilleker, D. G., & Vedel, T. (2013) "The Internet in Campaigns and Elections: The Oxford Handbook of Internet Studies". In Dutton, W. H. (ed.) *The Oxford Handbook of Internet Studies*. Oxford: Oxford University Press, 401–420.

Lilleker, D. G., Tenscher, J., & Štětka, V. (2015) "Towards hypermedia campaigning? Perceptions of new media's importance for campaigning by party strategists in comparative perspective", *Information, Communication & Society*, 18(7): 747–765.

Livingstone, S. (2009) "On the Mediation of Everything: ICA Presidential Address 2008", *Journal of Communication*, 59(1): 1–18.

Loader, B. D., & Mercea, D. (eds) (2012) *Social Media and Democracy: Social Media Innovations in Participatory Politics*. London: Routledge.

Lomicky, C. S., & Hogg, N. M. (2010) "Computer-Mediated Communication and Protest: An Examination of Social Movement Activities at Gallaudet, a University for the Deaf", *Information Communication and Society*, 13(5): 674–695.

López García, G. (2012) "Del 11M al #15M. Nuevas Tecnologías y Movilización Social en España", *Revista F@ro*, 1(16): 2–13.

López García, G. (2014) "Las Protestas de la #primaveravalenciana de 2012 y la #Intifalla: Medios, Redes y Ciudadanos", *Trípodos*, 34: 99–114.

López García, G. (2015) "Economic Crisis, New Media and New Political Structures. The Case of "Podemos": A Spanish 'Yes, We Can!' against the Two-Party System in Spain". Paper presented at IPSA Conference "Communication, Democracy and Digital Technology", Rovinj, Croacia, 2–3 October.

Lunt, P., & Livingstone, S. (2016) "Is 'Mediatization' the New Paradigm for our Field?", *Media, Culture & Society*, 38(3): 462–470.

Lyotard, J. F. (1984) *The Postmodern Condition: A Report on Knowledge*. Manchester: Manchester University Press.

Margolis, M., & Resnick, D. (2000) *Politics as Usual: The Cyberspace Revolution*. Thousand Oaks, CA: Sage.

Mattoni, A., & Treré, E. (2014) "Media Practices, Mediation Processes and Mediatization in the Study of Social Movements", *Communication Theory*, 24(3): 252–271.

Mazzoleni, G., & Schulz, W. (1999) "'Mediatization' of Politics: A Challenge for Democracy?", *Political Communication*, 16(3): 247–261.

McCombs, M. (2004) *Setting the Agenda: The Mass Media and Public Opinion*. Malden, MA: Polity Press.

McCurdy, P. (2012) "Social Movements, Protest and Mainstream Media", *Sociology Compass*, 6(3): 244–255.

McLeod, D. M. (2007) "News Coverage and Social Protest: How the Media's Protect Paradigm Exacerbates Social Conflict", *Journal of Dispute Resolution*, 1: 185–194.

McNair, B. (2006) *Cultural Chaos: Journalism, News and Power in a Globalised World*. London: Taylor & Francis.

Mertes, T., & Bello, W. F. (2004) *A Movement of Movements: Is Another World Really Possible?* New York: Verso.

Meyer, D. S., & Minkoff, D. C. (2004) "Conceptualizing Political Opportunity", *Social Forces*, 82(4): 1457–1492.

Micheletti, M. (2003) *Political Virtue and Shopping: Individuals, Consumerism and Collective Action*. New York: Palgrave.

Michels, R. (1998 [1915]). *Political Parties: A Sociological Study of the Oligarchical Tendencies of Modern Democracy*. New York: Transaction.

Micó, J. L., & Casero-Ripollés, A. (2014) "Political Activism Online: Organization and Media Relations in the Case of 15M in Spain", *Information, Communication and Society*, 17(7): 858–871.

Moffitt, B., & Tormey, T. (2014) "Rethinking Populism: Politics, Mediatisation and Political Style", *Political Studies*, 62(2): 381–397.

Monterde, A., Calleja-López, A., Aguilera, M., Barandiaran, X., & Postill, J. (2015) "Multitudinous Identities: A qualitative and Network Analysis of the 15M Collective Identity", *Information, Communication & Society*, 18(8): 930–950.

Morozov, E. (2011). *The Net Delusion: The Dark Side of Internet Freedom*. New York: Public Affairs.

Mouffe, C. (1995) "Post-Marxism: Democracy and Identity", *Environment and Planning D: Society and Space*, 13(3): 259–265.

Munck, G. L. (2006) "Monitoreando la Democracia: Profundizando un Consenso Emergente", *Revista de Ciencia Política*, 26(1): 158–168.

Munck, G. L. (2009) *Measuring Democracy: A Bridge Between Scholarship and Politics*. Baltimore, MD: Johns Hopkins University Press.

Muñoz Ramírez, G. M. (2008) *The Fire and the Word: A History of the Zapatista Movement*. New York: City Lights.

Muriel, E. (2014) "Cinco Claves del Éxito de la Campaña Electoral de Podemos", *La Marea*, 26 May. Retrieved from: www.lamarea.com/2014/05/26/cinco-cla ves-del-exito-de-la-campana-electoral-de-podemos/ (accessed 4 June 2015).

Murthy, D. (2011) "Twitter: Microphone for the Masses?", *Media, Culture and Society*, 33(5): 779–789.

Ordóñez, V., Feenstra, R. A., & Tormey, S. (2015) "Citizens against Austerity: A Comparative Reflection on Plataforma de Afectados por la Hipoteca (PAH) and Bündnis Zwangsräumung Verhindern (BZV)", *Revista Araucaria: Revista Iberoamericana de Filosofía, Política y Humanidades*, 7(34): 133–154.

Palao Errando, J. A. (2015a). "¿De qué Hablamos cuando Hablamos de Análisis del Discurso? Contra-hegemonía, Populismo y Mediaticismo en el Caso de Podemos", *Eu-topías*, 10: 35–46.

Palao Errando, J. A. (2015b). "La Enunciación Compleja: Hermenéutica, Semiótica y Política en el Siglo XXI. El Caso de Podemos". In Nos Aldás, E., Arévalo Salina, A., & Farné, A. (eds) *#Comunicambio 2015: Comunicación y Sociedad Civil para el Cambio Social*. Madrid: Fragua, 48–50.

110 *References*

Pérez Rioja, B. (2014) "El Streamer, entre el Periodismo Ciudadano y el Ciberactivismo". In Serrano, E., Calleja, A., Monterde, A., & Toret, J. (eds) *15MP2P. Una Mirada Transdisciplinar al 15M*. Barcelona: Tecnopolítica, 64–75. Retrieved from: http://tecnopolitica.net/libro15mp2p.

Perritt, H. H. (1997) "Open Government", *Government Information Quarterly*, 14(4): 397–406.

Pianta, M. (2013) "Democracy Lost: The Financial Crisis in Europe and the Role of Civil Society", *Journal of Civil Society*, 9(2): 148–161.

Pickard, V. W. (2006) "United yet Autonomous: Indymedia and the Struggle to Sustain a Radical Democratic Network", *Media, Culture and Society*, 28(3): 315–336.

Postill, J. (2014) "Democracy in an Age of Viral Reality: A Media Epidemiography of Spain's Indignados Movement", *Ethnography*, 15(1): 51–69.

Postill, J. (2015) "Field Theory, Media Change and the New Citizen Movements: The Case of Spain's 'Real Democracy Turn', 2011–2014". Retrieved from: https://johnpostill.com/2015/03/05/14-field-theory-media-change-and-t he-new-citizen-movements/ (accessed 4 June 2016).

Rancière, J. (2006a). "Democracia y Post-Democracia", *Ideas y Valores*, 98–99: 23–40.

Rancière, J. (2006b). *Hatred of Democracy*. London: Verso.

Rivero, J. (2014) *Conversaciones con Pablo Iglesias*. Madrid: Ediciones Turpial.

Robinson, A., & Tormey, S. (2005) "'Horizontals', 'Verticals' and the Conflicting Logics of Transformative Politics". In Hayden, P., & el-Ojeili, C. (eds) *Confronting Globalization*. London: Palgrave, 209–226.

Robinson, A., & Tormey, S. (2007) "Beyond Representation? A Rejoinder", *Parliamentary Affairs*, 60(1): 127–137.

Romanos, E. (2013) "Collective Learning Processes within Social Movements: Some Insights into the Spanish 15-M/Indignados Movement". In Flesher Fominaya, C., & Cox, L. (eds) *Understanding European Movements: New Social Movements, Global Justice Struggles, Anti-Austerity Protest*. New York: Routledge, 203–219.

Romanos, E. (2014) "Evictions, Petitions and Escraches: Contentious Housing in Austerity Spain", *Social Movement Studies*, 13(2): 296–302.

Rosanvallon, P. (2008) *Counter-Democracy: Politics in an age of Distrust*. Cambridge: Cambridge University Press.

Rucht, D. (2004) "The Quadruple 'A': Media Strategies of Protest Movements since the 1960's". In van de Donk, W., Loader, B., Nixon, P., & Rucht, D. (eds) *Cyberprotest: New Media, Citizens and Social Movements*. London: Routledge, 29–54.

Sampedro, V. (2015) "Podemos, de la Invisibilidad a la Sobre-Exposición", *Teknokultura*, 12(1): 137–145.

Sampedro, V., & Lobera, J. (2014) "The Spanish 15-M Movement: A Consensual Dissent?", *Journal of Spanish Cultural Studies*, 15(1–2): 61–80.

Sampietro, A., & Valera, L. (2015) "Emotional Politics on Facebook: An Exploratory Study of Podemos' Discourse during the European Election Campaign 2014", *Recerca*, 17: 61–83.

Saward, M. (2010) *The Representative Claim*. Oxford: Oxford University Press.

Saward, M. (2011) "The Wider Canvass: Representation and Democracy in State and Society. The Future of Representative Democracy". In Alonso, S., Keane, J., & Wolfgang, M. (eds) *The Future of Representative Democracy*. Cambridge: Cambridge University Press, 341–346.

Schudson, M. (1998) *The Good Citizen: A History of the American Civic Life*. New York: Martin Kessler.

Schumpeter, J. A. (2003) *Capitalism, Socialism and Democracy*. London: Routledge.

Shirky, C. (2009) *Here Comes Everybody: The Power of Organizing without Organizations*. New York: Penguin.

Shirky, C. (2011) "The Political Power of Social Media", *Foreign Affairs*, 90(1): 28–41.

Sifry, M. L. (2011) *WikiLeaks and the Age of Transparency*. New Haven, CT: Yale University Press.

Silverstone, R. (2007) *Media and Morality*. Malden, MA: Polity Press.

Sousa, A., Agante, P., & Gouveia, L. (2010) "Governmeter: Monitoring Government Performance: A Web-Based Application Proposal". In Andersen, K. N., Francesconi, E., Grönlund, A., & Van Engers, T. M. (eds) *Electronic Government and the Information Systems Perspective*. Amsterdam: Springer, 158–165.

Strömbäck, J. (2008) "Four Phases of Mediatization: An Analysis of the Mediatization of Politics", *The International Journal of Press/Politics*, 13(3): 228–246.

Strömbäck, J., & Esser, F. (2014) "Mediatization of Politics: Towards a Theoretical Framework". In Esser, F., & Strömbäck, J. (eds) *Mediatization of Politics: Understanding the Transformation of Western Democracies*. Basingstoke: Palgrave Macmillan, 3–28.

Stromer-Galley, J. (2014) *Presidential Campaigning in the Internet Age*. New York: Oxford University Press.

Subirats, J. (2011) *Otra Sociedad. ¿Otra Política?* Barcelona: Icaria.

Subirats, J. (2012) "Algunas Ideas Sobre Política y Políticas en el Cambio de Época: Retos Asociados a la Nueva Sociedad y a los Movimientos Sociales Emergentes", *Interface: A Journal for and about Social Movements*, 4(1): 278–286.

Sunstein, C. (2007) *Republic.com 2.0*. Princeton, NJ: Princeton University Press.

Tascón, M., & Quitana, Y. (2012) *Ciberactivismo: Las Nuevas Revoluciones de las Multitudes Conectadas*. Madrid: Catarata.

Tejerina, B., & Perugorría, I. (2012) "Continuities and Discontinuities in Recent Social Mobilizations: From New Social Movements to the Alter-Global Mobilizations and the 15M". In Tejerina, B., & Perugorría, I. (eds) *From Social to Political: New Forms of Mobilization and Democratization*. Bilbao: Argitalpen, 93–111.

Tewksbury, D., & Rittenberg, J. (2012) *News on the Internet: Information and Citizenship in the 21st Century.* Oxford: Oxford University Press.

Toret, J. (2015) "Una Mirada Tecnopolítica al Primer año de Podemos: Seis Hipótesis", *Teknokultura*, 12(1): 12–135.

Toret, J. (ed.) (2013) *Tecnopolítica: La Potencia de las Multitudes Conectadas. El Sistema Red 15M, un Nuevo Paradigma de la Política Distribuida.* Barcelona: Universitat Oberta de Catalunya.

Tormey, S. (2006) "'Not in My Name': Deleuze, Zapatismo and the Critique of Representation", *Parliamentary Affairs*, 59(1): 138–154.

Tormey, S. (2015a). *The End of Representative Politics.* Cambridge: Polity Press.

Tormey, S. (2015b). "Democracy Will Never be the Same Again: 21st Century Protest and the Transformation of Politics", *Recerca: Revista de Pensament i Anàlisi*, 17: 107–128.

Torreblanca, J. I. (2015) *Asaltar los Cielos: Podemos o la Política Después de la Crisis.* Barcelona: Debate.

Torres Rodríguez, L. (2015) "La Tuerka: Un Modelo de Tertulia Política en una Televisión Comunitaria". In Candón-Mena, J. I. (ed.) *Move.Net: Actas del I Congreso Internacional Move. Net sobre Movimientos Sociales y TIC.* Sevilla: Grupo Interdisciplinario de Estudios en Comunicación, Política y Cambio Social de la Universidad de Sevilla (COMPOLÍTICAS), 328–346. Retrieved from: https://idus.us.es/xmlui/handle/11441/44109.

Tufekci, Z. (2013) "'Not This One': Social Movements, the Attention Economy, and Microcelebrity Networked Activism", *American Behavioral Scientist*, 57(7): 848–870.

van Biezen, I., Mair, P., & Poguntke, T. (2012) "Going, Going ... Gone? The Decline of Party Membership in Contemporary Europe", *European Journal of Political Research*, 51(1): 24–56.

Van Laer, J., & Van Aelst, P. (2010) "Internet and Social Movement Action Repertoires: Opportunities and Limitations", *Information, Communication and Society*, 13(8): 1146–1171.

Verba, S., & Nie, N. (1972) *Participation in America: Political Democracy and Social Equality.* New York: Harper & Row.

von Beyme, K. (2011) "Representative Democracy and the Populist Temptation". In Alonso, S., Keane, J., & Merkel, W. (eds) *The Future of Representative Democracy.* Cambridge: Cambridge University Press, 96–123.

Webb, P., Farrell, D., & Holliday, I. (2002) *Political Parties in Advanced Industrial Democracies.* Oxford: Oxford University Press.

Weber, M. (1978) *Economy and Society.* Berkeley, CA: University of California Press.

Wessels, B. (2011) "Performance and Deficits of Present-Day Representation". In Alonso, S., Keane, J., & Merkel, W. (eds) *The Future of Representative Democracy.* Cambridge: Cambridge University Press, 50–73.

Whiteley, P. F. (2011) "Is the Party Over? The Decline of Party Activism and Membership across the Democratic World", *Party Politics*, 17(1): 21–44.

Žižek, S. (2001) *Repeating Lenin*. Zagreb: Arkzin. Retrieved from: www.lacan. com/replenin.htm.

Žižek, S. (2010) "From Democracy to Divine Violence". In Agamben, G. (ed.) *Democracy in What State?* New York: Columbia University Press, 100–119.

Index